Praise

Complete

lead book in the Loving Jesus w...

"Engaging and soulful."
—PUBLISHER'S WEEKLY

"Shannon Ethridge's life exhibits God's transforming power. Her response to tragedy will guide others who struggle through dark valleys, to find the light of hope that is in Christ."
—MAX LUCADO, best-selling author

"When the worst has happened, only time can bring perspective and turn trauma into triumph. Shannon Ethridge is an incredible woman who has a story to tell and a passion to share. Through experiences that would level most, she has risen as a lover of Jesus who can speak to the heart of every woman. *Completely His* calls even the most timid or scarred to a place of deep, sweet relationship with the One who patiently waits for His beloved to lean in and trust Him. I loved the book. I love Shannon's heart."
—JAN SILVIOUS, author of *Foolproofing Your Life* and *Big Girls Don't Whine*

"Insightful and daring, *Completely His* so challenged me to look at myself honestly and ask 'Am I *all* yours, God?' Shannon is completely vulnerable as she shares a longing for God in every area of her life and a step-by-step example of how to walk with Him in all aspects of daily living. This message is encouraging, life changing, and much needed by every one of us."
—SHAUNTI FELDHAHN, best-selling author of *For Women Only* and *For Men Only*

Other books by Shannon Ethridge

Completely His
Completely Loved
Every Woman's Battle
Every Woman's Battle Workbook
Every Young Woman's Battle
Every Young Woman's Battle Workbook
Every Single Woman's Battle
Every Woman, Every Day
Every Woman's Battle Promise Book
Preparing Your Daughter for Every Woman's Battle
Every Woman's Marriage
Every Woman's Marriage Workbook
Words of Wisdom for Women at the Well
Words of Wisdom for Well Women

LOVING JESUS
A 30-DAY GUIDE
WITHOUT LIMITS

COMPLETELY
Forgiven

Responding to God's Transforming Grace

SHANNON ETHRIDGE

Best-selling author of the Every Woman's Battle series

WATERBROOK
PRESS

COMPLETELY FORGIVEN
PUBLISHED BY WATERBROOK PRESS
12265 Oracle Boulevard, Suite 200
Colorado Springs, Colorado 80921
A division of Random House Inc.

ISBN 978-1-4000-7112-8

Library of Congress Cataloging-in-Publication Data
Ethridge, Shannon.
    Completely forgiven : responding to God's transforming grace / Shannon Ethridge.—1st ed.
        p. cm.
    ISBN 978-1-4000-7112-8
    1. Christian women—Prayers and devotions. 2. Forgiveness of sin—Meditations. I. Title.
    BV4844.E83 2007
    242'.2—dc22

                                                                    2007003305

Printed in the United States of America
2007—First Edition

10 9 8 7 6 5 4 3 2 1

CONTENTS

AN INVITATION INTO
THE GRACE OF GOD

*H*ave you ever wondered how God could possibly love you after all you've done? Me too. Especially since He knows everything about us—even the shortcomings we fail to see ourselves. As scary as that thought may seem, we have absolutely no reason to fear. Why? Because God says the same thing to us today as He did to Paul two thousand years ago:

> My grace is sufficient for you, for my power is made perfect in weakness. (2 Corinthians 12:9, NIV)

Sufficient. God said His grace was sufficient for the likes of the radical, prejudiced, persecuting, Christ-hating, terroristic murderer we now know as the apostle Paul—the man through whom God wrote the majority of the New Testament. But is it possible that God's grace is sufficient for the likes of me and you as well? Absolutely, because God's magnificent power is made all the more perfect in (not in spite of) our weakness.

Since you are holding this book in your hands, I hope it means what I think it means—that you have found the study of God's Word to be as addictive as I warned it would be in the first devotional, *Completely Loved*. However, if this is the first book you've picked up in the Loving Jesus Without Limits series, let me explain how it works. This devotional is the second in a series of four that accompany the lead book, *Completely His*. If you've not read it yet, I encourage you to do so for a look at how God is wooing and pursuing you as His spiritual bride. But if you choose to read this book first, you'll still be enriched by it—and the three other devotionals in the series. That's because each one is designed to help you dive into God's Word for yourself, taking you into a deeper level of commitment to your heavenly Bridegroom, Jesus Christ.

Imagine how different life could be when you experience thirty days of heart-to-heart time with God through this book, and then thirty more days through another devotional in the series, and so on, all the while learning more and more about:

- how far God has gone to reveal Himself to us and draw us closer (the message in *Completely Loved: Recognizing God's Passionate Pursuit of Us*)
- how God can use us mightily in spite of our shortcomings (the message of the devotional you are holding)
- how God lavishes both His presence and His presents on us (explored in *Completely Blessed: Discovering God's Extraordinary Gifts*)
- how our love for God cannot be contained but can be shared naturally (examined in *Completely Irresistible: Drawing Others to God's Extravagant Love*).

The first devotional focuses on God's interactions with people in the Bible to give you a clearer glimpse into His character and His pursuit of us. This one takes a closer look at some of those saints and sinners, as well as God's reaction to them. In their stories we'll find answers to some of our deepest questions about how we are to live, questions such as:

- Does anyone else have the kinds of struggles and temptations I have?
- Is God going to give up on me someday? After all, my spiritual life seems to be two steps forward, three steps back!
- How can I avoid some of the more subtle yet destructive sins so common to people?
- Is it possible to live out the righteousness that Christ offers?

It's only natural that, as human beings, we have questions like these. The good news is that God has answers in His Word, and He's not just willing to reveal them to you—He's eager to do so!

As you read this devotional, I hope you'll come to understand that Christ's death on the cross has thoroughly cleansed you. In His eyes, you are as pure as you can possibly be. There's nothing more you can add to Christ's sacrifice and nothing more you can do to earn higher standing with God. You are completely forgiven. No loopholes. No disclosures. No fine print on the contract. God's grace is simply all you need. I call this *positional purity.*

In addition to the positional purity God has already bestowed on you, I hope you'll be inspired to pursue what I call *experiential purity* as well. I pray you'll want to respond to His lavish love and grace by living out your right-eousness, not so you can achieve a legalistically pure life, but in order to experience the freedom and joy that comes from living according to His desires for His people. When you are committed to living a lifestyle pleasing to God, you will be transformed, both inside (with your heart and mind) and outside (with your actions). This transformation will not only bring God great glory, but it will also bring you great pleasure, satisfaction, peace, and happiness as you live the abundant life you were meant to live.

Over the next thirty days, you'll read about squabbling siblings, great patriarchs and matriarchs, royalty and royal failures, conquerors and concu-bines, builders of God's kingdom, and builders of their own kingdoms. We'll focus on what their actions and choices tell us about how to live a life that is more holy and pure and that genuinely reflects God Himself. Then by answering the introspective questions at the end of each reading called "Holding His Hand," you'll gain a clearer picture of how you can respond to God's transforming grace and live out the righteousness that you have already received.

Imagine the freedom that will come as a result of recognizing that you are completely forgiven. You won't have to worry about God's disapproval anymore. You won't have to wear yourself out trying to make up for past failures. You won't have to obsess over earning spiritual brownie points. You can know God's favor is on your life and even learn to love yourself simply because God loves you and because His grace is sufficient—even for the likes of you and me.

So if you are ready to respond to your invitation into the grace of God, let's get started.

THE WISDOM
OF REMAINING
IGNORANT

Daily reading: Genesis 2:4–3:24

Key passage: The LORD God placed the man in the Garden of Eden to tend and care for it. But the LORD God gave him this warning: "You may freely eat any fruit in the garden except fruit from the tree of the knowledge of good and evil. If you eat of its fruit, you will surely die." (Genesis 2:15–17)

*O*ur family was driving from Texas to Alabama during the month of August, and we decided to take a break at a rest stop somewhere in Arkansas. Fifteen-month-old Erin had been incredibly fussy while strapped in her car seat, so we stopped to let her run around for a while, even though it was almost one hundred degrees outside. Kids must have a built-in radar for cool water on a hot day, as Erin toddled directly toward a candy cane–shaped waterspout several yards away. Knowing what she was thinking,

I ran after her, hoping to keep her from getting her clothes soaked, but she cried hysterically when I swept her up in my arms. My daughter didn't want Mommy to rescue her. She had her heart set on getting wet.

There weren't many people near, so I just did what any merciful mother would do for her baby on a sweltering day. I stripped Erin naked and let her run wild underneath that flowing waterspout. My daughter frolicked unashamedly for half an hour while I laughed and snapped all the pictures I could—what a Kodak moment! I thought, *Oh, how wonderful it would be if I could turn back the clock and feel that innocent and uninhibited again!*

I couldn't help but wonder if Adam and Eve felt something similar as they were banished from their idyllic paradise, wearing their new clothes and knowing they could never again return to the days of unashamed nakedness and innocence. God had placed them in a perfect environment, without a need or concern in the world. All they had to do was enjoy the lush garden and its wildlife, each other, and God. They had nothing to worry about, nothing to fear. God wanted it that way. The only restriction He had put on them pertained to one particular tree: "You may freely eat any fruit in the garden except fruit from the *tree of the knowledge of good and evil*" (Genesis 2:16–17). God didn't want Adam and Eve to have knowledge of both good and evil. He only wanted them to have knowledge of good.

However, their curiosity got the best of them. One minute they were thinking, *Hmm… I wonder what would happen if I took a bite of that forbidden fruit?* A short time later, they were wishing they didn't know the answer to that question. If only they could rewind the tape and have a "do over," but the damage was done, and the ripple effect of their sin would rock every one of our boats from that time forward.

Adam and Eve's sin was that they wanted to know *more* than God wanted them to know, and they searched for that knowledge apart from God. This is the essence of much of our sin as well. Sometimes we want to know things that we'd be much better off not knowing. For example:

- Susan heard a rumor that Cheryl's husband had divorced her over a decade ago because she had cheated on him. Susan asked around, and word got back to Cheryl about it. "If you really felt you needed to know, why didn't you come and ask me directly, instead of asking other people?" Cheryl asked.

  Devastated by how she had hurt her friend, Susan wished she'd never heard the rumor in the first place, or that she would have just ignored it and not inquired about it further. Whether it was true or not didn't matter as much as the loss of her friend's trust.

- In her early sixties, Belinda is dying of lung cancer. She had her first cigarette at age fourteen, simply because she was curious as to what smoking would be like. One smoke led to another, and soon she was hooked. She now says, "If only I had never smoked that first cigarette. I wish I had known they were so addictive, but it's too late for that now."

- When Marla's boyfriend, Tom, admitted he was not a virgin, Marla said she was okay with that (because she wasn't either). However, she pressed him for more information—how many partners he'd been with, who they were, and where they had their encounters. Tom thought he was doing the right thing by answering all her questions, but too much information caused Marla to become jealous and insecure since she knew many of his past lovers. Their relationship crumbled as a result.

Bruised friendships… enslaving addictions… jealousy and insecurity. Sometimes our curiosity can lead us where we don't really want to go. But it doesn't have to, especially if we remember that peace and happiness don't come from knowing everything, as God does, but from simply obeying God and trusting Him to reveal information on a need-to-know basis. His goal is not to keep things *from* us, but to hold certain information *for* us so it doesn't cause unnecessary pain and suffering in our lives.

HOLDING HIS HAND

Am I the kind of person who feels she has to know everything about everyone? If so, what have I learned from today's reading?

_____

_____

_____

_____

Do I believe there is wisdom in remaining unaware of certain situations, especially when I am powerless to help the person involved or make any real difference? Am I content not to know things I don't necessarily need to know? Why or why not?

_____

_____

_____

_____

How might I be guarding myself and my loved ones by not pressing for information they don't want to share with me?

_____

_____

_____

_____

Can I trust God to reveal information to me on a need-to-know basis? Why or why not?

_____

_____

_____

_____

Dearest God,

How Your heart must have broken when Adam and Eve sought the knowledge that You wanted to protect them from. Reveal to us the ways in which we are guilty of the same thing. Keep us from sinning against You and against others with our unnecessary curiosities and hurtful gossip. Show us the wisdom in remaining ignorant, helping us guard our minds from gathering "too much information." We trust that You will reveal to us things that we truly need to know. Amen.

A TOWER
OF TROUBLE

Daily reading: Genesis 9:1; 11:1–9

Key passage: Let's build a great city with a tower that reaches to the skies—a monument to our greatness! This will bring us together and keep us from scattering all over the world. (Genesis 11:4)

I fondly recall my visits to my paternal grandmother's home every summer because she always spoiled me rotten. The summer before my fourth-grade year, however, I learned that Mawmaw wasn't always about spoiling, but also about strict discipline when necessary.

One day I asked her if I could walk over to the clubhouse before dinner so I could get some exercise (something I needed as a pudgy, prepubescent girl). Mawmaw responded, "You may go, but you are not allowed to buy candy out of the vending machine." *Is she a mind reader?* I wondered. *How does she know that's why I want to go for a walk?*

"Yes, ma'am," I responded. Then I walked over to the clubhouse, dug thirty-five cents out of my pocket, and plugged the coins into that vending machine without a second thought. My favorite candy bar was Bit-O-Honey, but I wouldn't have time to chew it all before getting back to the house, so I pressed B-5, and down dropped a bright yellow bag of peanut M&M's. I ripped open the package, put it to my lips, and scarfed down the bite-sized pieces of candy. On the way home I disposed of the evidence in a trash can and brushed my teeth upon arrival to make sure there was no chocolate on my breath. As soon as I came out of the bathroom, my grandmother asked, "Did you go to the candy machine?"

"No, ma'am," I lied. That's when I found out she had spies all over that housing complex.

"I called my friend who works at the reception desk, and she told me that you walked out of the clubhouse eating candy," she said. Busted. But I figured all I'd get was a wink, a grin, and a "Don't do that again." After all, she was my sweet Mawmaw, and I was her "precious little grand-dor-ter," as she frequently called me. I was shocked to find out, however, that Mawmaw would not tolerate my lying.

She sternly explained my sentence. "You will not get any of my chocolate pie tonight since you've already had your dessert. And do you know that special picnic we were going on tomorrow with your friends to Dennis the Menace Park? We won't be going. You'll stay in your room instead." I cried for at least an hour over how Mawmaw had confounded my fun plans, thinking she'd perhaps give in. She never budged, however, and I never disobeyed or lied to her again.

Rather than respecting my grandmother's authority over me and obeying her rules, I assumed that I could get away with my actions without her knowledge, or that there would be no consequences to pay even if she did find out. I was wrong—and so were the people who, in spite of God's commandment to "multiply and fill the earth" (Genesis 9:1), insisted on doing their own thing.

The descendants of Noah wanted to stay together and resisted being scattered all over the world. They wanted to build a cultural hub with a magnificent tower reaching to the heavens. But God stepped in and confounded their plans to build such a city. Why? Because they were supposed to spread out all over the earth and make a name for God in every part of the world, not stay together and make a name for themselves with an extravagant piece of architecture.

If we think pride like this doesn't exist anymore, we'd better think again. People in just about every field—science, medicine, law, politics, education, and even religion—believe they can make a name for themselves by ignoring God's sovereign existence and doing their own thing. For example, Darwinists confidently claim that we naturally evolved from apelike creatures. Scientists claim with confidence that the world was created by a big, random cosmic bang. Liberal lawmakers use "separation of church and state" as an excuse to try to make it illegal for students to pray in public schools or for judges to publicly display the Ten Commandments in their courthouses. Researchers are harvesting human fetuses and experimenting with cloning, all in the name of science, disregarding the sanctity of human life. Legislators recently allowed the removal of a feeding tube from a vegetative human because they (in the place of God) deemed that her life was subpar. Where is our fear of God? Surely, He will once again confound those who seek to steal His glory and undermine His sovereignty.

How about you? Do you respect God's sovereignty over everything, including you? Living out your righteousness includes obeying His commands. He knows what's best for you—after all, He made you and knows you better than you know yourself! Of course, you'll stumble and fall into sin on occasion, but when you do, do you quickly acknowledge that you are outside of God's will? Do you wholeheartedly seek restoration? Do you make a conscious effort to choose humility over humiliation?

May it always be so for you and for me, lest we, like the architects of Babel, find ourselves in a tower of trouble with our plans and aspirations confounded.

HOLDING HIS HAND

When I look at how I spend my time each day (working at home, in an office, in a classroom, and so on), what are two or three reasons why I do the things I do?

_____

_____

_____

Do these reasons line up with my purpose in life of being a clear reflection of the God who made me? Am I trying to make His name great or my own name great?

_____

_____

_____

What adjustments might I need to make in order to ensure that the motives behind my daily missions are positive, God-honoring ones?

_____

_____

_____

Precious Jesus,

Your name and Your works are truly matchless! There is no way we can compare even one aspect of our lives with Your infinite importance and greatness. Thank You for showing us true humility and submission, Lord. Keep pride far away from our hearts and minds. Amen.

THE DECEIVER AND
THE DESPISER

Daily reading: Genesis 25:19–34; 27:1–28:9; 32:1–33:17

Key passage: "Look, I'm dying of starvation!" said Esau. "What good is my birthright to me now?"

So Jacob insisted, "Well then, swear to me right now that it is mine." So Esau swore an oath, thereby selling all his rights as the firstborn to his younger brother. Then Jacob gave Esau some bread and lentil stew. Esau ate and drank and went on about his business, indifferent to the fact that he had given up his birthright. (Genesis 25:32–34)

*I*f ever there were severe cases of sibling rivalry, we see them in the pages of Genesis, especially between Jacob and his big brother, Esau.

As the firstborn twin, Esau possessed the family birthright, which meant he was the family leader just beneath his father. It also meant that Esau was entitled to double the inheritance of his younger brother, Jacob.[1] However, this all seemed to mean little to Esau, as he sold his birthright to Jacob for nothing more than some bean soup and bread. You would think that as soon as Esau's hunger pangs returned a few hours later, he would regret what he'd done, yet Scripture tell us that he was "indifferent" (Genesis 25:34). Translation: Esau couldn't give a hoot about his birthright. His apathy spat in the face of his father's legacy.

Esau's regret finally surfaced when he realized that not only did Jacob bargain his birthright away from him, but his brother also stole their father's blessing. Oh, how Esau wept, wailed, and lamented that his father did not have even one blessing left for him because of Jacob's deception! But Esau's regret didn't lead him to repentance. Instead, it led him to vengeance. Esau plotted to kill his brother, hoping to regain or at least avenge his birthright and blessing. He also added to his rebellion against his father by marrying one of the Canaanite women his father detested. If Esau's earlier apathy spat in his father's face, this act was an additional slap across the cheek.

Lest you think that all the tension and rivalry between the two brothers was necessary in order to fulfill the prophecy that "the older will serve the younger" (Genesis 25:23, NIV), think again. All the deception, betrayal, and real-life drama was manufactured by human hands, not God's. The strife resulted from Jacob's desire for power and Esau's disrespect toward God. Jacob wanted to inherit the spiritual heritage; Esau didn't. Both got what they wanted. Deception is never a necessary element in God's plan, nor is hardness of heart. God accomplished His will, not because of the brothers' sin and strife but, rather, in spite of it. Yes, God can do anything He desires, even through deceivers and despisers, such as Jacob and Esau.

However, God wasn't finished with these two yet. He eventually mended the fence that separated them, bringing the two together for a memorable reunion. In Genesis 32, we witness Jacob humbly approaching Esau, fully expecting vengeance and retaliation for his deception. However, God honors Jacob's prayers for protection from his older brother (see verse 11). Esau approaches him with hundreds of men, not to strike him down, but to safeguard Jacob and his family on their journey. Esau has had years to reflect on his attitude toward his father, his brother, and his God, and we see that God has indeed blessed him as well as Jacob. His father's prophecy is fulfilled: "You will serve your brother for a time, but then you will shake loose from him and be free" (Genesis 27:40). Through forgiveness, Esau is freed from his hard heart toward his brother.

It may be difficult to imagine that anyone would act as Esau did, but the spirit of hardheartedness is still alive and well. I recently heard a woman say that her husband resents it when she reads her Bible, especially if they are on vacation. While he should be thankful for a godly wife, he seems to despise her attempts to grow spiritually. Another woman once mentioned that she feels her husband gives too much money in the offering plate at church. She seemed to resent his generosity toward God. I've not been exempt either. I regrettably remember shouting at my mother, "Stop that noise!" as she was singing hymns in the kitchen. God has certainly used the past two decades to soften my heart toward my mother and to make me so very appreciative of the rich spiritual heritage she has passed down to me.

What about you? Do you spur on your family and friends toward love and good deeds, or do you find yourself feeling hardhearted toward some? Do you value other people's faith in God, or do you sometimes resent them for it? Are you indifferent to your family's faith, or do you celebrate it?

Do yourself a favor, dear friend, and embrace your spiritual heritage. Live to love and serve God, and love and serve His people wholeheartedly. In doing so, God will be able to bless older and younger believers *through* you, rather than in spite of you.

HOLDING HIS HAND

Do I truly value the spiritual heritage handed down to me by my ancestors? Why or why not?

_____

_____

_____

Do I carry bitterness in my heart toward someone, even another believer? If so, who is it, and what is it that I seem to despise about that person?

_____

_____

_____

How can I release my negative feelings toward others? What do I need to let God do in me to soften my heart and help me live out my righteousness in Christ?

_____

_____

_____

Dearest God,

What a rich spiritual heritage we have, one that's been passed down to us through many generations of believers. Teach us to value and pass on this precious gift of faith, Lord. Help us to soften our hardened hearts so that we are not robbed of the joy that is our inheritance as followers of Christ. Amen.

THE GREAT BABY RACE

Daily reading: Genesis 29:1–30:24; 35:16–26; 49:29–33

Key passage: So Jacob slept with Rachel, too, and he loved her more than Leah. He then stayed and worked the additional seven years.

But because Leah was unloved, the LORD let her have a child, while Rachel was childless.…

When Rachel saw that she wasn't having any children, she became jealous of her sister. "Give me children, or I'll die!" she exclaimed to Jacob.

Jacob flew into a rage. "Am I God?" he asked. "He is the only one able to give you children!" (Genesis 29:30–31; 30:1–2)

To say that the stress at Jacob's house was high is a major understatement. Intending to marry one sister, Jacob was tricked into marrying both. The younger sister was loved; the older unloved. Score a point for Rachel, the younger. But the unloved sister got pregnant and had the first child. Score a point for Leah. In fact, score four points for Leah, since she bore Jacob four sons (Reuben, Simeon, Levi, and Judah) before Rachel had a child.

In a jealous fit, Rachel told Jacob to impregnate her maid, since Rachel was barren (are you having flashbacks to Jacob's grandparents, Sarah and Abraham?). Score two for Rachel, as her maid, Bilhah, gave birth to Dan and Naphtali. Refusing to be outdone, Leah resorted to the same shenanigans and gave her maid, Zilpah, to her husband. Draw two more points on Leah's side of the scoreboard with the birth of Gad and Asher to Zilpah.

One day Leah's son Reuben brought his mother mandrake plants, and Rachel asked for some. Leah didn't take too kindly to Rachel's inquiry, and out of her mouth spewed years' worth of bitterness and jealousy. "Wasn't it enough that you stole my husband? Now will you steal my son's mandrake roots, too?" Leah asked (Genesis 30:15). So Rachel struck an irresistible bargain; she swapped her man for some mandrakes. She agreed that Leah could sleep with Jacob that night in exchange for the plants. (Mandrakes were believed to enhance one's fertility, thus the brouhaha.) Leah was the beneficiary of the bargain, as she eventually scores three more points with the births of Issachar, Zebulun, and finally a daughter, Dinah.

In time, however, the Lord remembered Rachel's plight and gave her a son. Rachel named him Joseph and asked for another (30:22–24). Sometime later she also gave birth to Benjamin, but she died during the delivery. The final score in the Baby Race was Rachel 4, Leah 8.

Although Rachel was Jacob's first and only true love, it was ultimately Leah who was buried beside Jacob and his ancestors. And although Jacob clearly favored Rachel's son Joseph over all the others, it was Leah's son Judah through whom the lineage of Christ would flow. Rachel won Jacob's love. Leah won Christ's lineage. But my feeling as I read this story again and again is that both sisters lost a great deal.

When I was four, my eight-year-old sister died suddenly, leaving me lonely for that intimate female companionship that we shared for the first four years of my life. Growing up without a sister led me to believe that if she had lived, we'd have surely been best friends. I hope I wouldn't have let any petty comparisons or competitions separate me from Donna.

I imagine that perhaps Leah and Rachel were once good friends. Growing up in the same household, they probably slept in the same room, picked wildflowers in the field together, styled each other's hair, wore each other's clothes, and whispered their secrets to each other. Yet they allowed jealousy to destroy the bond they had shared as sisters. They became embroiled in the battle to outdo each other, causing life to become a bitter race that produced no real winner.

May I ask you something? Has jealousy destroyed vital relationships in your life? Do you look at special people as God's gift to you, or do you look at the ways you don't measure up to them? Do you recognize how God has blessed others and therefore give Him praise, or do you see the many things others have but you don't? Or worse, do you consider yourself better than others based on how God has blessed you more? Pride can separate brothers and sisters in Christ as easily as envy.

If we look at life as a race against one another, we'll all end up losers for sure. Remember, we are all on the same team. We are all children of God, and He doesn't play favorites. Although we may receive different blessings at different times in our lives, God has enough gifts to go around. He doesn't take from one in order to give to another. So pursue holiness by rejoicing with others in what they have, and trusting in God to fulfill the desires of your own heart.

HOLDING HIS HAND

Have I allowed comparison and competition to destroy a relationship with someone who used to be near and dear to me? If so, what can I do to restore that closeness?

_____

_____

_____

How do I think God feels about His beloved children bickering, bartering, and jockeying for position as Leah and Rachel did? Why?

_____

_____

_____

How can I guard my heart against growing bitter toward someone who may appear to be more blessed in some way?

_____

_____

_____

How can I avoid growing prideful toward someone who appears to be less blessed somehow?

_____

_____

_____

Heavenly Father,

It must break Your heart to provide for Your children so abundantly, only to have them competing and comparing themselves to one another. Give us hearts of gratitude for what we have, hearts of thanksgiving for what others have, and spirits of love and respect toward all our brothers and sisters in Christ. Amen.

A BROTHER'S
KEEPER—OR KILLER?

Daily reading: Genesis 4; Hebrews 11:1–4; 1 John 3

Key passage: We must not be like Cain, who belonged to the evil one
and killed his brother. And why did he kill him? Because Cain had been
doing what was evil, and his brother had been doing what was right....

If we love our Christian brothers and sisters, it proves that we have
passed from death to eternal life. But a person who has no love is still
dead. Anyone who hates another Christian is really a murderer at heart.
And you know that murderers don't have eternal life within them. We
know what real love is because Christ gave up his life for us. And so we
also ought to give up our lives for our Christian brothers and sisters.
(1 John 3:12, 14–16)

Cain and Abel were brothers, one a farmer and the other a shepherd.
Both brought their first fruits as offerings to God, yet God only
looked upon Abel's with favor, not Cain's. While we may assume that God
simply prefers beef over beets, each of these two offerings was appropriate. It

is only natural that a farmer would offer produce while a shepherd would offer livestock. So, there had to be something more that differentiated these two offerings.

Although scholars debate the cause of God's rejection of Cain's offering, my interpretation of this passage is that Cain's attitude toward the Lord wasn't what it should have been when making an offering. We only see Cain and Abel's outward actions, but God was looking into their hearts, and He apparently didn't like what He saw in Cain's. God rebuked Cain, saying, "Why are you so angry?... Why do you look so dejected? You will be accepted if you respond in the right way" (Genesis 4:6–7).

Rather than feeling repentant when God rebuked him, Cain's hardness of heart soon led him to sin more, even after God warned him that this would be the case: "But if you refuse to respond correctly, then watch out! Sin is waiting to attack and destroy you, and you must subdue it" (Genesis 4:7).

What in Cain's heart caused the Lord such displeasure? One can only speculate, but based on what transpires as the story progresses, my guess is that Cain envied his brother. Perhaps he felt that Mom and Dad liked Abel better. Maybe Abel seemed like a goody two-shoes most of the time, and, in contrast, Cain looked like the black sheep. Perhaps Cain thought Abel didn't have to work as hard tending to his animals as he did tending to his crops. We'll never know the reason this side of heaven, but what we do know is that Cain's envy and hatred drove him to do the unthinkable—to kill his own brother.

To make matters worse, Cain lied to God. When the Lord inquired about Abel's whereabouts (as if He didn't know already), Cain replied, "I don't know.... Am I my brother's keeper?" (Genesis 4:9, NIV).

Whoa. Poor choice of words when you are talking to the Creator and Sustainer of the universe. God cursed Cain so he was no longer able to live off the land. Cain began to whimper like a dog with its tail between its legs. He couldn't stand the thought of becoming a restless wanderer, and he feared that someone would kill him. If I had been God, I probably would have sarcastically replied, *"Oh, you poor dear! My heart bleeds a peanut-butter-and-jelly sandwich for you! What's wrong, Cain? You can dish it out, but you can't take it?"*

However, in spite of Cain's heinous murder and bald-faced lies, God somehow found a tender spot in His heart for him. He placed a special mark on Cain so that no one could kill him and then allowed him to find a wife and raise a family. I find it amazing how God can still have mercy on even the hardest of criminals!

Not only does God have enough mercy for Cain, but He also has more than enough mercy for you and me. Perhaps you, like Cain, have a sibling (or someone else in your life) who seems to be able to do everything right, causing you to feel like you do everything wrong. Or maybe you envy other people because of what they are doing for God. Rather than rejoice over how God has blessed them, you are jealous instead, wondering, *Why doesn't God bless me like that?* Or maybe you've eagerly anticipated the beautiful and talented soloist hitting the wrong note or stumbling and falling head over heels as she descends from the stage. Rather than cheering her on to perform her best for God, you have privately hoped she would fail somehow.

Regardless of who you've been envious of, or why, know that God wants you to master your jealousy before it progresses into even more destructive emotions. Let's focus on offering our personal best to God (including a humble heart) while encouraging others to do the same.

HOLDING HIS HAND

Have I ever envied another person because of her gifts or talents? If so, who was it, and what was the real reason I felt the way I did?

When I make an offering to the Lord, do I compare it to what others are able to do and become jealous of those who are able to do more? Why or why not?

If God can have mercy on a cold-blooded killer like Cain, do I believe that He has enough mercy for me, too? Why or why not?

Heavenly Father,

We know Your love and mercy are genuine, but so often our jealousy and anger prevent us from showing Your love and mercy toward our brothers and sisters in Christ. Forgive us when we fall prey to this sin, and give us repentant hearts that sincerely celebrate the accomplishments and offerings of others. Amen.

PRIDE AND PREJUDICE

Daily reading: Acts 10:1–11:18

Key passage: Then Peter replied, "I see very clearly that God doesn't show partiality. In every nation he accepts those who fear him and do what is right." (Acts 10:34–35)

---

*C*ornelius must not have fit the typical Gentile mold of his era, for the Bible commends him for his devotion and fear of the Lord, his prayer life, and his financial gifts to the poor (see Acts 10:2). We meet this unusual Roman when an angel of the Lord visits him and instructs him to send men to Joppa to get Simon Peter.

The very next day, Peter has a vision of a sheet being lowered from heaven, holding all kinds of animals (both clean and unclean), and a voice telling him to, "Get up, Peter; kill and eat them" (Acts 10:13). Peter was a devout Jew who strictly abided by the Jewish dietary laws not to eat any unclean animal, so the command repulses him. "Never!" he replies.

But the voice sets Peter straight, saying, "If God says something is acceptable, don't say it isn't" (Acts 10:15). When he has the same vision two more times, Peter starts to wonder about the meaning of the visions. The Holy

Spirit tells him that three men are looking for him and that he is supposed to go with them.

Still uncertain of the visions' meaning, Peter agrees to go with the three men and travels the significant distance to Cornelius's house, where he discovers he has a large, captive audience. In talking with Cornelius about why he was sent for, Peter finally realizes God's purpose in the visions: to bring Jews and Gentiles together under one umbrella of God's grace.

In Jesus' day, Jews had many rules and regulations about Jew-Gentile relations. One of the biggest no-nos was for a Jew to eat with a Gentile. Not only were their dietary laws very different, but Gentiles did not tithe, so Jews were forbidden to accept their hospitality.[1] In fact, Jews were so prejudiced against Gentiles that they considered them to be outsiders to God's plan of salvation.

The time was ripe for Gentiles to hear the good news of Jesus' death and resurrection and to have an invitation extended to become followers of Christ. God wanted Jews and Gentiles to know that His grace is for everyone, and He chose Cornelius and Peter to demonstrate this, first to each other, then to the church, and finally to the world.

When Peter realizes what God is trying to communicate to him through the triplicate vision, his Jewish pride melts. He is stripped of his prejudices against the Gentiles as he realizes that the message in the visions was that God's love for the Gentiles is as great as His love for the Jews. Peter preaches the good news of the gospel to everyone gathered at Cornelius's house, the Holy Spirit comes upon the Gentiles, and they are baptized as followers of Christ. Many generations of racial prejudice against the Gentiles came to an end during this encounter, and the early church recognized these new converts as Christians without requiring that they become Jewish.

Sadly, this kind of pride and prejudice still exists today, between Jews and Gentiles, blacks and whites, believers and nonbelievers, and many other groups. In fact, a few years ago I became aware of a prejudice I didn't know I had, and God humbled me over it.

The year was 1998, and we had recently moved from the big city of Dallas to the East Texas country town of Lindale. I had promised my kids that we'd get a couple of dogs when we moved to the country, so on this particular day I was making good on my promise. Later, I was going to do some painting, so I threw on some old denim overalls that morning. My late-model minivan was in the shop, so the only vehicle available was our farm truck, a 1972 bright blue Ford F-150. We picked up the puppies—a black Lab and a Blue Heeler—then headed toward home.

On the way, I realized I needed to pick up some dog food, so I stopped at the first store I could find. That's when it hit me. *Yikes! I'm sitting in the parking lot of the Dollar General store, wearing overalls and driving an old, beat-up pickup truck with a gun rack in the window and two dogs in the back! I have become one of them! If my Dallas friends saw me now, they'd think I was a* red-neck *for sure!*

While this particular realization was more of a joke than a real conviction, there have been times when I've sensed an ugly pride welling up in me as I'm tempted to look down my nose at someone whose appearance, values, or lifestyle is different than mine. But then I realize, *Who am I to think I am any better than anyone else?*

If the truth be known, we all have a little pride and prejudice lurking in us somewhere. God's message to Peter two thousand years ago applies to us today, particularly if we want to live out our righteousness in Christ. Whether Jew or Gentile; red, yellow, black, or white; redneck or city slicker, we all have the same thing in common—a desperate need for God's grace.

HOLDING HIS HAND

How does this story affect my view of God?

_____

_____

_____

Is there a group of people I feel superior to for some reason? If so, who are they, and why do I feel the way that I do?

_____

_____

_____

What are the results of pride and prejudice in my life? Do they really *set me apart* or simply *tear me apart* from relationships with other human beings? Why?

_____

_____

_____

> *Father God,*
>
> *We acknowledge that Your intention was for all to come under Your umbrella of grace. None of us is better than our brothers and sisters who may have a different color of skin or speak with a different dialect. Teach us to see the good (and the God) in one another and to value each other as You value us. Amen.*

LASTING IMPRESSIONS

Daily reading: Acts 4:32–5:11

Key passage: Then Peter said, "Ananias, why has Satan filled your heart? You lied to the Holy Spirit, and you kept some of the money for yourself. The property was yours to sell or not sell, as you wished. And after selling it, the money was yours to give away. How could you do a thing like this? You weren't lying to us but to God." (Acts 5:3–4)

When I was a youth pastor, a young girl wanted to share her favorite "original poem" with me. As I tried to decipher the scribbled words in her journal, "Lead me on to a place where the river runs into your keeping…" they seemed vaguely familiar. Then I recognized them as the lyrics to the Amy Grant song "Lead Me On."[1] I began singing the song and asked the girl if she had ever heard it. I could tell by the nervous look on her face that the similarities weren't coincidental. I suspected she was trying to impress me. Her dishonesty had the opposite effect.

She wasn't the first—or the last—teen whose strong desire to make a positive impression led them to make unimpressive choices. I remember one time when our youth group was setting up for a large banquet in the fellowship hall. With only a few hours to go before the event, I left the kids with instructions to "get all the tables and chairs set up quickly!" I was tending to other matters, going back and forth between my office and the pastor's, passing by the fellowship hall each time. Several times I heard the kids griping, "Come on, Ben! Shannon said we all had to help. Stop clowning around." A short while later I returned to check on the progress. Most of the kids had gone outside for a break, but Ben was playing his Game Boy all by himself. As I looked around the room, Ben announced, "I've got it under control! The room is all set up just like you said!" But I knew Ben hadn't done much of the work. He just wanted me to think he had.

Have you ever wanted to make a great impression on someone? Sure, we all have. But have you wanted to impress someone so badly that you misrepresented yourself, lying in order to make yourself look better than you really are? Unfortunately, many of us have that tendency in common with today's Bible characters, Ananias and Sapphira.

Before we talk about their hypocrisy, let's back up and take a look at one of their fellow church members, Barnabas. At the close of the fourth chapter of Acts, the believers are freely sharing their possessions with one another, making sure there are no poor among them and that everyone is taken care of. It was in this spirit that Barnabas sold a piece of property and presented 100 percent of the proceeds at the feet of the church leaders. Barnabas must have been praised, although desire for praise doesn't appear to be his reason for the charitable contribution.

But it certainly appears to be Ananias and Sapphira's motivation. What proof do we have that they were driven by a desire to make a good impression and be praised? They lied. They sold the land for one price, held back a portion of the proceeds, then conspired together to present the rest of the money as if it were 100 percent of the sale price. They didn't want anyone to know they had personally profited from the sale.

Understand that Ananias and Sapphira were under no obligation to sell their land or to donate any of the money. Believers were doing this strictly out of the goodness of their hearts. It wasn't that Ananias and Sapphira were being coerced into selling and were holding back what they thought was rightfully theirs. They could have simply said, "We sold a piece of property, and we'd like to donate this much of the proceeds." Their gift still would have been a significant charitable act received with gratitude.

So why did they feel the need to lie? They wanted to impress the leaders and church members with their supposed generosity. But their hypocrisy—and God's judgment—made a much bigger impression than their generosity.

Of course, the lasting impression on their church wasn't made with their good deed, but with their grave sites. Word spread quickly about this couple's folly and fate, and the believers took it as a sign from God that He will not be lied to. I'm thankful that God is far more merciful today than He was when He was making an example of Ananias and Sapphira. If church members were still struck dead every time they were greedy, dishonest, or hypocritical, the church would be a funeral home.

But just because God is merciful doesn't mean we shouldn't strive to avoid these sins. After all, He sees not just everything we do but every motive behind our actions. We needn't worry about making a lasting impression upon anyone—other than Him. By concerning ourselves with God's opinion of us rather than other people's, we'll be in a position to live open-book lives before everyone, thus properly responding to God's transforming grace.

HOLDING HIS HAND

Do I worry too much about what other people think of me? Why or why not?

_____

_____

_____

Have I ever tried to make a good impression at the cost of my integrity? If so, how do I feel about that now? What do I wish I had done differently?

_____

_____

_____

How can I live an open-book life with myself, my church leaders, and God? Are there hidden sins I need to confess in order to have a clean conscience and be in right relationship? If so, what might God be prompting me to do to remedy the situation?

_____

_____

_____

Precious Lord,

There is no person on the planet so important that we have to lie in order to impress them. Yours is the only approval we need, so we invite You to search our hearts, purify our motives, and help us act with the utmost of honor and integrity in every situation. Amen.

WHEN TEMPERS
FLARE

Daily reading: Numbers 22:1–38; John 2:13–25; Ephesians 4:17–32

Key passage: "Don't sin by letting anger gain control over you." Don't let the sun go down while you are still angry, for anger gives a mighty foothold to the Devil. (Ephesians 4:26–27)

*B*alaam was a prophet, but don't be fooled into thinking he had anything in common with the prophets of the living God. He was actually a pagan diviner (similar to a fortune-teller) who read signs from animals to determine the will of the gods. The king of Moab had called upon Balaam to determine the will of the God of Israel, but the king's goal was for Balaam to manipulate God into cursing Israel rather than blessing her. He wanted to make sure that the Israelite army did not overtake his own army (see Numbers 22:4–7). Of course, Balaam's mission was doomed before it began. Here's how the story plays out.

While riding toward Moab, Balaam sees that something is troubling his donkey, but he can't see the angel standing in front of them, wielding a sword.

Out of fear of the angel and to protect his master, the donkey shies away three times. Balaam responds by exploding and beating the donkey each time, claiming the donkey has "made a fool of [him]" (Numbers 22:29, NIV).

I can just imagine Balaam's veins popping out on his forehead as he beats that poor animal. I can also imagine his jaw dropping as the donkey opens its mouth and speaks. Talk about a clear sign from God! Balaam has no doubts that it's the Lord who is speaking to him, telling him that he should only speak the words that God puts in his mouth—words of blessing for Israel rather than curses. While Balaam thought he could manipulate Israel's God, God showed him otherwise.

Fast-forward many Scripture pages and many centuries, and see Jesus in the temple, along with lots of cattle, sheep, and doves. There are also several money-changers, and there were coins passing back and forth between those who had come to offer their sacrifices to God and those who were looking to make a profit from the piety of others. Jesus doesn't take too kindly to what is going on in His Father's house. These animals aren't merely being made available as a service to those who wished to make sacrifices; the chief priests have turned the temple courts into a marketplace, where lots of money can be made.

Can't you just imagine Jesus charging through the scene, flipping over tables and sending animals and coins flying? Some money-changers tremble and run for cover amid the chaos, while others scramble to gather up spilled coins from the ground before they're lost or stolen. They aren't concerned about protecting the sanctity of God's temple. They are only concerned about the sale of their goods and the cash flow it will create for them.

Both these stories involve scared, bewildered animals and overwhelming anger, but Balaam's anger and Jesus' anger couldn't be more different. You see, Balaam was infuriated because his donkey wasn't serving his own purposes. Balaam's was a selfish, abusive anger. Jesus, on the other hand, was infuriated because the chief priests were not serving His Father's purposes, and the money-changers were not fulfilling His Father's agenda. His was a controlled, selfless, appropriate anger—a righteous indignation that He had every right to feel, for He was passionately guarding His Father's interests.

If we want to live a pure life, we cannot allow our anger to cause us to sin (see Ephesians 4:26). Keep in mind that anger as an emotion is not wrong. Every human being experiences it to some degree. It's what we do with our anger that determines whether we are acting selfishly or selflessly. For example, when my children deliberately disobey me, I have a right to be angry about that. Properly channeled, my controlled anger can lead me toward disciplining them in a loving and appropriate way. However, improperly channeled, my uncontrolled anger can lead me to yell at them, belittle them, or discipline them too harshly.

We have every right to be angry over injustices in our world, such as innocent victims harmed by drunk drivers or child molesters. Indeed, we should allow our anger to move us toward social action. We don't have the right, however, to angrily take the law into our own hands and kill someone whom we know is a drunk driver or a child molester. Paul encourages us in the book of Romans to, "Hate what is wrong. Stand on the side of the good.... Never avenge yourselves. Leave that to God. For it is written, 'I will take vengeance; I will repay those who deserve it,' says the Lord" (12:9, 19).

What about you? Do you channel your anger appropriately? Do you allow it to move you toward productive action, as Jesus' did? Or does your anger cause you to sin, as Balaam's did? Don't let your anger go unchecked, for it can quickly cause great damage, hindering your relationships with the object of your anger and, most of all, with God.

The next time you feel your blood pressure go up, your face turn red, and your veins pop out because of anger, take a moment to ask yourself, *Why am I feeling this way? Is it for a selfish reason or a righteous reason? Is an injustice truly being done here, or am I just not getting my own way?* Most importantly, consider how you can vent your anger without sinning. In doing so, you'll represent your heavenly Bridegroom well.

HOLDING HIS HAND

Who or what makes me angry most often? Why?

_____

_____

_____

How do I typically respond when I am angry with this person or situation? Is my reaction justifiable or just plain selfish?

_____

_____

_____

What might God be telling me today through this devotional? Do I need to evaluate or change my behavior when I feel angry? If so, how?

_____

_____

_____

Father God,

We were created in Your image; therefore we were given the emotion of anger for a reason. Yet we often use it just to manipulate situations and get our own way. Help us not to sin in our anger, but rather allow it to lead us to appropriate action, for we truly want to represent You well. Amen.

NOAH'S BIG NO-NO

Daily reading: Genesis 9

Key passage: After the Flood, Noah became a farmer and planted a vineyard. One day he became drunk on some wine he had made and lay naked in his tent. Ham, the father of Canaan, saw that his father was naked and went outside and told his brothers. Shem and Japheth took a robe, held it over their shoulders, walked backward into the tent, and covered their father's naked body. As they did this, they looked the other way so they wouldn't see him naked. (Genesis 9:20–23)

The Bible stories we heard about Noah as we were growing up included an ark, a flood, and animals coming two by two, but my Sunday-school teachers never mentioned the darker part of Noah's life. I first read about Noah getting drunk when I was an adult. I was shocked to discover that the righteous evangelist God spared from the flood would do such a thing.

I have to say, though, that I was relieved to discover this story in the pages of my Bible. It's not that I wanted Super-Noah to trip on his cape and commit some terrible sin so he'd lose his status as a great spiritual hero. I'm glad because

Noah teaches us that even the godliest of people are not immune to temptation, even after achieving great spiritual victories. His story also gives us hope to know that even when we stumble and fall, God doesn't forsake us.

We sometimes believe we should be living every day as perfect Christians once we step forward and profess our faith in Christ. But you and I both know how difficult perfection is to achieve. In fact, it's impossible. Does that make us less Christian? No, it certainly doesn't. In the words of a Bob Carlisle song, "Saints are just the sinners who fall down and get up."[1]

Remember, our faith isn't based on our own ability to be good. It's based on God's ability to cleanse us when we prove to be not so good. As Christians, we are to strive to be sinless, but we will most likely fail over and over again. And over and over again, we face the decision—will we stay down, or will we stand back up?

Did you notice how God responded to Noah's drunkenness and nakedness? We don't see Him canceling the covenant He had made with Noah, nor do we see Him disqualifying Noah from service. We don't even see Noah getting a tongue-lashing from an angel. Instead, we see God using Noah's sin as an opportunity to reveal the true character of each of his three sons.

One of Noah's sons, Ham, exposes his father's nakedness, and because Ham shames his father, Ham's future generations are cursed. Noah's other two sons, Shem and Japheth, are blessed because they drape a garment across their shoulders and walk into their father's tent backward so as to cover him without laying eyes upon his naked body.

What a beautiful picture of grace! Shem and Japheth weren't interested in getting an eyeful of their father's shame. They wanted to protect him from even further disgrace. Their actions remind us that "love does not delight in evil" (1 Corinthians 13:6, NIV) and "love covers all offenses" (Proverbs 10:12).

So the next time you find yourself facedown in sin, remind yourself that once you're completely forgiven, God sees you as righteous, regardless of whether you are facedown or standing upright. I pray this knowledge will inspire you to recognize that you don't have to stay down. You can get up, dust yourself off, and approach God with confidence that you, like Noah, will be granted mercy (see Hebrews 4:15–16). Also know that God, in His sovereignty, can use your sin to teach you things about Himself, yourself, and those around you, if you are willing to look at the situation with a teachable spirit.

Finally, when you see someone else lying facedown in sin, which course of action will you choose? Will you expose her sin and shame, or will you lovingly strive to reclothe her with dignity, honor, and grace? Part of living a pure life is looking out for those who are facedown when you are standing upright. With God's help, we can all stand and walk in righteousness together.

HOLDING HIS HAND

Has my indulgence in alcohol or some other substance brought sin and shame upon me and my family? If so, how?

_____

_____

Do I believe with all my heart that I am still a chosen saint of God even when I stumble and fall into sinful behavior? Why or why not?

_____

_____

Am I willing to do unto others as I would have them do unto me, covering their sin and shame with grace rather than exposing them to others? How can I do this if the need arises?

_____

_____

_____

Most merciful Father,

It's hard for us to imagine that You, being so very perfect, can sympathize with our many imperfections. Thank You for showing us in Your Word that no spiritual hero was perfect in every way except Christ Himself. Help us strive for perfection yet willingly receive (and offer) grace whenever necessary. Amen.

WHO'S LAUGHING NOW?

Daily reading: Genesis 17:15–18:15; 21:1–7

Key passage: Then the LORD did exactly what he had promised. Sarah became pregnant, and she gave a son to Abraham in his old age. It all happened at the time God had said it would.... Abraham was one hundred years old at the time.

And Sarah declared, "God has brought me laughter! All who hear about this will laugh with me." (Genesis 21:1–2, 5–6)

---

*A*ccording to the November 4, 2004, issue of the *New England Journal of Medicine,* doctors recommend that women wanting to get pregnant should do so before they are forty-five years of age. Beyond that, their fertility is significantly decreased, and the health risk to both mother and child increases.[1]

Now suppose you are twice that age, and three strangers tell you that you'll be holding your own biological child within a year. Almost seems like a cruel joke, doesn't it? But this was the position Sarah found herself in at ninety years of age. Can you imagine the disappointment she must have felt over being childless, decade after decade, despite God's earlier promise that Abraham's offspring would be as numerous as the stars (see Genesis 15:5)?

The shame she must have endured day after day, particularly after Abraham fathered a son, Ishmael, with Sarah's servant, Hagar (see Genesis 16)? Remember, in that culture a woman's infertility was considered a curse from God.

Then God once again tells Abraham that He is going to make him the father of many nations and that Sarah is going to have his child. In response, Abraham falls to the ground in worship, yet is laughing to himself at the incredibility of God's statement. Abraham assumes that this is an impossibility and asks that his son, Ishmael, receive God's blessing instead, but God makes it clear that the blessing will come through Sarah's child, not Hagar's. Scripture doesn't satisfy our curiosity as to whether Abraham informed Sarah of what God said. My guess is that he didn't want to get her hopes up, just in case he had heard God wrong.

But three visitors make the same announcement within earshot of Sarah as she is in the tent preparing food for them. Sarah responds by laughing to herself as well. Even though her laughter is silent, the Lord (who is represented by the three visitors) hears it, turns to Abraham, and questions, "Why did Sarah laugh? Why did she say, 'Can an old woman like me have a baby?' *Is anything too hard for the LORD?* About a year from now, just as I told you, I will return, and Sarah will have a son" (Genesis 18:13–14).

Both Abraham and Sarah laughed at the notion, but God rebuked only Sarah. We don't know why, but perhaps their laughter came from different spirits. Or maybe Abraham laughed because, although God's plan was seemingly impossible, he knew full well that God could fulfill the plan if He willed it. We get the impression that Sarah's response came from a doubting heart. Surely she had prayed over and over that God would give her a child, yet month after month, year after year, her prayers went unanswered. She must have doubted that God would give her a child, even if He could, and her laughter demonstrated that doubt. She seemed to have forgotten that God purposefully promised to give her and Abraham their own biological child and that He always fulfills His promises.

When God confronted her, Sarah denied her laughter. He gently rebutted, "That is not true. You did laugh" (Genesis 18:15).

I can just imagine the Lord with a smile and a raised eyebrow, thinking, *Just you wait, Mrs. Sarah. I'll show you what I am capable of, and we'll see who's laughing then!* Initially, Sarah was most likely laughing *at* God when considering the notion that she could still have a child. But in His mercy and lovingkindness, God opened her womb, causing Sarah to laugh *with* Him instead. Sarah moved from barren to blessed, as she and Abraham celebrated the birth of their long-awaited son and the heir of God's promises to the nation of Israel.

What about you? Do you believe that God will do for you the things He says He will? Do you believe that if you have confessed your past mistakes and sins and received His forgiveness, you are now pure and sinless in His sight? That when He sees you, He sees a pure and spotless bride? That He is returning to claim you as His own at the wedding supper of the Lamb?

Or are there things that you don't even bother asking God for because you consider them too difficult? I confess there have been people, situations, and relationships that I've thought were too far gone for any good to come of them. I've pessimistically accepted the idea that some things are simply beyond hope. Rather than pray in faith, believing that all things are possible with God, I've fallen prey to the temptation just to shake my head and tsk-tsk them right out of my mind. However, this story of Sarah's doubt and renewed faith is a powerful reminder that nothing is beyond God's abilities—absolutely, positively nothing!

Is there something that you have laughed to yourself about, thinking it impossible even for God to accomplish? More important, have you allowed your doubt to hinder your boldness and confidence in approaching Him in prayer to ask for your own personal miracle in accordance with His will? If so, take a lesson from Sarah and Abraham. Even if you've laughed at the notion in the past, have faith that God can deliver whatever you ask according to His will. And when you receive your own special miracle, rejoice and laugh *with* God rather than at Him.

HOLDING HIS HAND

Like Sarah, have I doubted that God could or would do something in my life or in the lives of others? What was it, and why did I assume the situation was beyond hope?

_____

_____

_____

Does our personal lack of faith change anything about God's abilities to do miracles? Why or why not?

_____

_____

_____

What does our lack of faith say about our own personal belief in God? What does our confident faith say about our belief in God?

_____

_____

_____

Faithful God,

Help us learn to always trust You rather than doubt You. Although we may have silently laughed at You in the past, thinking You'd never give us a particular miracle, we ask Your forgiveness. Please do for us what You did for Sarah— give us cause to laugh with You as You show us Your mighty miracle-working power. In Jesus' most holy and precious name. Amen.

WILL THE REAL DECEIVER PLEASE STAND UP?

Daily reading: Genesis 38; Matthew 1:1–3

Key passage: About three months later, word reached Judah that Tamar, his daughter-in-law, was pregnant as a result of prostitution. "Bring her out and burn her!" Judah shouted.

But as they were taking her out to kill her, she sent this message to her father-in-law: "The man who owns this identification seal and walking stick is the father of my child. Do you recognize them?"

Judah admitted that they were his and said, "She is more in the right than I am, because I didn't keep my promise to let her marry my son Shelah." But Judah never slept with Tamar again. (Genesis 38:24–26)

---

*a*t first glance, one may think what Tamar did was inexcusable—hiding her identity, posing as a prostitute, and agreeing to sleep with her father-in-law. If this happened today, the scandal would surely make the headlines of the *National Enquirer*. But our cultural norms are very different from those in Tamar's day.

When Tamar became a widow, tradition required that her brother-in-law step up to the plate and serve as a sire or stud of sorts. So when Tamar's husband, Judah's oldest son, Er, was struck down by God for his wickedness, it was Onan's responsibility to marry and impregnate Tamar so she could bear a child who would become his brother Er's heir. But Onan knew that the child would be his brother's legal heir rather than his own, so he didn't want to fulfill the role. Instead, he had sexual relations with Tamar but spilled his semen on the ground so he wouldn't impregnate her. God didn't take too kindly to Onan's shirking his responsibility, so God struck Onan dead as well.

Judah was left with only one son, Shelah. While Judah promised Shelah to Tamar once Shelah grew up, Judah had no intention of allowing Shelah to marry Tamar. Judah didn't want to run the risk of losing that son too. Perhaps Judah thought that the cause of his two evil sons' deaths was the "curse of Tamar" rather than the curse of God.

Even though Judah was shirking his own responsibilities of ensuring his family lineage by withholding Shelah, Tamar took Jewish law far more seriously. Even though she had married and lost not one but two wicked husbands from the same family, she was bound and determined to bear a child from this family's seed. If Judah wouldn't betroth her to Shelah, then Judah would have to fulfill the responsibility himself. Indeed he did, but in such a way that *he* received the disgrace, not his daughter-in-law.

First Judah deceived Tamar. Then Tamar deceived Judah. Yet God still worked through these deceitful individuals. As we read in the first chapter of Matthew, Tamar is a vital link in the lineage of Jesus. Her sinful approach to upholding Jewish laws didn't disqualify her from Jesus' family tree, for God remains faithful to His promises. Judah, too, is included in the lineage of Jesus, even though he failed to be a man of his word. Don't you just love that about God? He blesses us, not because we always do what is right, but because He always remains true to His word.

Now let's move this story closer to home. How important is it to you to be a woman of your word? When you tell somebody that you will do something or be somewhere, do you make every effort to fulfill your promise? Are you known for being trustworthy? Or do people frequently have reason to doubt you, even when you say you'll do something, because of how you've failed to live up to your word in the past?

Remember when we were kids, if we doubted someone's word, we might say, "Do you promise? Do you swear? Do you pinkie swear? No take backs!" Perhaps the person responded with words like, "Cross my heart, hope to die, stick a needle in my eye if I don't!" Now that we are adults, people shouldn't have to ask us if we promise to do something. The fact that we say we will should be enough. In fact, Jesus told His disciples, "Do not swear at all: either by heaven, for it is God's throne; or by the earth, for it is his footstool; or by Jerusalem, for it is the city of the Great King. And do not swear by your head, for you cannot make even one hair white or black. Simply let your 'Yes' be 'Yes,' and your 'No,' 'No'; anything beyond this comes from the evil one" (Matthew 5:34–37, NIV).

As the bride of Christ, we represent our Bridegroom—His holiness, His purity, His honesty, His loyalty, His resolve to be true to His word. Let's live out our righteousness by being women of our word as well.

HOLDING HIS HAND

When I tell someone I am going to do something, do I make every effort to do it, even if it becomes a burden or inconvenience? Why or why not?

_____

_____

_____

Can I remember a time when someone told me she was going to do something, but then she didn't? If so, how did that make me feel?

_____

_____

_____

How can I avoid making someone else feel that way? Do I need to go back to someone I've made a commitment to and be honest with her about my ability (or inability) to remain true to that commitment?

_____

_____

_____

Precious Lord,

You remain so true to Your word! You are the epitome of truth and holiness. Help me become a woman of my word as well, being careful not to overcommit myself, misrepresent my intentions, or disappoint anyone due to a lack of trustworthiness. Amen.

TIES THAT BIND

Daily reading: Joshua 2; 6:15–25

Key passage: Before they left, the men told her, "We can guarantee your safety only if you leave this scarlet rope hanging from the window.... We swear that no one inside this house will be killed—not a hand will be laid on any of them. If you betray us, however, we are not bound by this oath in any way."

"I accept your terms," she replied. And she sent them on their way, leaving the scarlet rope hanging from the window. (Joshua 2:17–21)

*N*ot long ago I was flipping through the channels on our television and came across a woman in tears. Her lovely face was downcast, and she had a difficult time looking the interviewer in the eye. As she told her story, she explained how her husband had left her with four young children and that she had no education to speak of. Her career opportunities were extremely limited, with the exception of one of the oldest occupations in the world—prostitution.

Sadly, this woman felt her only chance of survival was to become a prostitute in her own home while her children slept in their rooms. For over three years, she had worked her "trade" several nights each week while putting herself through community college. Eventually she was able to get a steady job that provided just enough money to pay the bills and feed her kids without her selling her body.

It had been over two years since this woman had been involved in prostitution, yet her self-esteem was still in the gutter. I could almost see the scarlet letter *A* she was subconsciously wearing on her forehead. With a quivering chin and eyes full of tears, she claimed, "I'm all used up." After all she had done, she felt she had nothing left of herself to offer anyone, especially God.

My heart broke for this woman, and I wished I could tell her the story of Rahab. When God needed to enlist the aid of a trusted individual who could deliver the city of Jericho into Israel's hands, He didn't look to a prophet or a priest, but to a prostitute. Even though Rahab had spent perhaps years servicing male clients with her body, she still had the character and courage to offer her service to God.

If you think about it, a prostitute was an ideal choice to fulfill the role of protector for Israel's spies. Where else could men hang out without suspicion from the neighbors or the city officials? Surely they had seen strange men come in and out of Rahab's house for years.

Rahab seemed to know a great deal about both the history and the future of Israel. She knew that God would be faithful to usher them into the Promised Land, even at the expense of her own city. Given her eagerness to side with the Israelites in this battle, she must have seen the takeover as imminent. And heroically, Rahab chose to risk her life by committing treason, deceiving her own people in order to protect the Israelite spies. If discovered, she would have immediately been put to death.

Joshua realized the tremendous sacrifice this woman was making on Israel's behalf. His spies promised that she and her family would be spared from the destruction if she would keep their deal a secret, keep her family in the house during the battle, and keep a scarlet cord hanging in the window to show the soldiers which house to protect. Can you imagine the commander of a mighty army trusting a prostitute to collaborate with him in such a way? Surely, the favor of the Lord was on Rahab and her family.

It may be tempting to assume that Rahab was simply going through the necessary motions to save her own skin, but there's something more than self-preservation going on here. Rahab and her family embraced the company of the Israelites, and it appears that afterward the Israelites adopted her family. In fact, the first chapter of Matthew reveals that Rahab is also included in the lineage of Jesus Christ. She married a man named Salmon, gave birth to Boaz, and eventually became King David's great-great-grandmother. Can you believe that Jesus had prostitutes in His family tree? It's true. Believe it.

I wonder, have you ever felt as if you are all used up with nothing left to give God? Do you think you've become so deeply entrenched in sin that you've been disqualified from God's service? If so, please meditate on this— *God's favor and honor aren't* awarded *based on your actions; nor are His favor and honor* removed *because of your actions.*

In other words, God isn't so concerned with what you've done in the past. He's more concerned with who you are becoming in the future. You are completely forgiven, set free from your past, and equipped to live confidently as the chosen bride of Christ.

HOLDING HIS HAND

Have my past actions led me to believe that I've been disqualified from service to God? If so, why do I feel this way?

_____

_____

_____

_____

Can I earn God's favor by being good? Can I lose God's favor by being bad? Why or why not?

_____

_____

_____

_____

If I turn my back on my past and strictly look ahead to my future, who do I see myself becoming? What am I allowing the Lord to do in my life that will lead me to be more of a reflection of Him in the future?

_____

_____

_____

_____

Lord Jesus,

You can choose anyone You want to accomplish Your will, yet You so often choose the least likely candidate to bring You honor and glory. Repeat history, and use my life the way You used Rahab's. Strategically position me such that I can offer all that I am to reveal all that You are. Amen.

I DID IT MY WAY

Daily reading: Exodus 17:1–7; Numbers 20:1–13

Key passage: But the LORD said to Moses and Aaron, "Because you did not trust me enough to demonstrate my holiness to the people of Israel, you will not lead them into the land I am giving them!" This place was known as the waters of Meribah, because it was where the people of Israel argued with the LORD, and where he demonstrated his holiness among them. (Numbers 20:12–13)

---

*A*s a little girl, I remember adults on numerous television shows imitating Frank Sinatra singing, "I did it my way!"[1] While doing it his own way may have worked great for Frank, it failed miserably for Moses.

As the chosen leader and intercessor between the Israelites and God, Moses's primary responsibility was to be God's mouthpiece. When God told Moses to jump, he was supposed to respond, "How high?" He was to do everything God said to do, exactly the way God said to do it. No making assumptions, no second-guessing, no inserting his own agenda. It had to be God's way all the way.

While this arrangement worked for the first thirty-nine years the Israelites were in the desert, the plan went awry when Moses was only one year away from completing the "forty years of wandering" sentence and leading his people into the Promised Land. What caused Moses to suddenly do things his way instead of the Lord's way? I suspect it was an excuse that many churches (and individuals) use today—"But we've *always* done it *that* way!"

Not that Moses had a long history of bringing water out of rocks, but he did have some previous experience in his earliest days of leadership. In Exodus 17, we see God instructing Moses to strike the rock at Meribah with his staff in order to bring forth water to quench the people's thirst. Mission accomplished, Houston. We have water, and we have peace, at least for now.

But thirty-nine years later, the people are again thirsty. They have no rain or river, but they do have a rock, a rock that God specifically told Moses to "speak to" (Numbers 20:8, NIV) in order to bring forth water. Although Moses had stuttered in the past, God never did. His directions were clear. Speak to it, Moses. Use your words, not your weapon.

But what does Moses do? He resorts to old data saved in his memory bank rather than relying on the new data God had just given him. Rather than speaking to the rock, he strikes it with his staff, not once, but twice, as if God's way wouldn't have worked. Perhaps he was thinking, *I've always done it this way! It worked last time, didn't it? Do what works! If it's not broke, don't fix it!*

However, God hadn't instructed Moses to strike the rock with his staff. Moses's actions didn't simply reflect a minor mental lapse or a senior moment. His action exposed his new attitude, most likely brought about by the constantly complaining crowd. It was an attitude of independence, self-reliance, and even rebellion. His disobedience brought negative consequences: he wouldn't be allowed to enter the Promised Land after all those years of faithful leadership.

What can we learn from Moses's mishap at Meribah? I think it is this: when God gives us leadership responsibilities, we aren't to take them lightly, nor are we to do things our way. We can't take God's place; we are merely His representatives. We must fulfill our heavenly Bridegroom's agenda, not our own. We must seek His fresh guidance daily, then do things His way, rather than our way or even old ways that have worked in the past.

I learned the truth of this firsthand in 1998. In *Completely His*, I tell the story of how I clearly heard God say, "Move here," when I accidentally wound up in Lindale, Texas. The Realtor we contacted showed us places both in and around Lindale, and one of the places we looked at was a quaint little farmhouse on several acres of land in the neighboring town of Van. Desperate to escape the inappropriate relationship that tempted me in Dallas, we immediately put a bid on the house. Mentally, emotionally, and spiritually we were already living in that little house. We were eager to move in physically as well.

A few weeks later (after we had already sold the house we were living in), we got a call from the Realtor, saying that the seller had decided to take the house off the market and keep it in the family. Shocked and devastated, we turned to God, asking, "How could You let this happen?"

He responded, "I never told you to move to Van. I told you to move to Lindale." We were saddened to realize that in our eagerness, we had taken the reins from God and had begun galloping in our own direction rather than in the direction He had clearly spelled out for us. We repented and asked God to guide us exactly to where He wanted us, and He promptly led us to this wonderful log cabin in Lindale. Every time I drive by that farmhouse in Van, I thank the Lord that He didn't let me do things my way, but rather that He showed us His way.

What is your preferred mode of operation? Do you tend to want to do things your way? If so, I encourage you to give it up, girlfriend. Let go of your mirage of control, and ask God to lead you His way instead.

HOLDING HIS HAND

Have I ever tried to do things my way rather than God's way? If so, when was it, and what was the outcome?

How often do I pause and ask God for confirmation or denial that I am on the right track when it comes to obeying His voice? Do I feel this is an important thing to do? Why or why not?

If I were to consistently ask God for guidance and do things exactly the way I sensed Him directing me, what effect would it have on my life? On the lives of those around me?

Most holy God,

You created me and strategically placed me on earth with a purpose and a plan for my life. However, I confess that I often try to take control and develop my own plans. Forgive me for the ways that I attempt to be self-sufficient, and restore me to the path that You have prepared for me. Amen.

SOMEONE'S IN THE BEDROOM WITH DINAH

Daily reading: Genesis 34; Romans 12:17–21

Key passage: Never pay back evil for evil to anyone. Do things in such a way that everyone can see you are honorable. Do your part to live in peace with everyone, as much as possible.

Dear friends, never avenge yourselves. Leave that to God. For it is written, "I will take vengeance; I will repay those who deserve it," says the Lord. (Romans 12:17–19)

*B*ig brothers have earned a reputation for two things: picking on their little sisters, and protecting them when necessary. In Dinah's case, she had several older brothers, yet they must not have been around the moment that Shechem, a Canaanite, laid his lustful eyes on their sister's beautiful body. Shechem forces himself on Dinah and decides he has to have her as his wife. After raping her, he begs his daddy to go and negotiate a bride price for her. Dinah is curiously silent throughout this entire story, so we can only imagine how she must have felt being raped and then having her rapist beg for her hand in marriage.

When Dinah's brothers get wind of the situation, their hearts break for their sister, and their fury rages toward Shechem and his father, Hamor. But the brothers forget that two wrongs don't make a right. When Shechem and Hamor beg the Israelites to intermarry with their clan, Dinah's brothers devise a vengeful plan. They pretend to be interested in the proposal, provided all the men of the clan are willing to be circumcised.

Let's take a quick commercial break for a little history lesson: circumcision was the sign that set the Jews apart from all the other people on earth. It was a symbol of the covenant they had made with God to be His chosen people. At least three times we see Israel's forefathers and mothers fearing the day when the Israelites intermarried with other tribes:

- "One day Abraham said to the man in charge of his household, who was his oldest servant, 'Swear by the LORD, the God of heaven and earth, that you will not let my son marry one of these local Canaanite women. Go instead to my homeland, to my relatives, and find a wife there for my son Isaac'" (Genesis 24:2–4).

- "Then Rebekah said to Isaac, 'I'm sick and tired of these local Hittite women. I'd rather die than see Jacob marry one of them'" (Genesis 27:46).

- "So Isaac called for Jacob, blessed him, and said, 'Do not marry any of these Canaanite women. Instead, go at once to Paddan-aram, to the house of your grandfather Bethuel, and marry one of your uncle Laban's daughters'" (Genesis 28:1–2).

To this day, most Orthodox Jews forbid their children to marry outside the Jewish faith. They feel a duty to remain set apart as God's chosen race.

This, then, is the cultural milieu into which Shechem and Hamor make their proposal that not only should Shechem marry Dinah, but the Israelites and Canaanites should be allowed to intermarry freely. And it's not just the Israelite women that the Canaanites are interested in, but their abundant property and numerous herds as well. Hamor and Shechem amiably suggest to the brothers, "You may live among us; the land is open to you! Settle here and trade with us. You are free to acquire property among us" (Genesis 34:10), but in speaking to the townsmen about the matter, they plot that, "all their flocks and possessions will become ours" (Genesis 34:23). Israel's holy inheritance is at stake here. If the brothers agree to these terms, they've just sold the Israelite family farm right along with their sister. They would actually be erasing the line that distinguishes the Israelites from all others.

Of course, the brothers' agreement is just a ruse in order to weaken the men so they can take even greater advantage of them than Shechem took of their sister, Dinah. Once Hamor, Shechem, and all of the men are circumcised (and painfully sore as a result), Simeon and Levi slaughter every male inhabitant and plunder the city.

But rather than commend his sons for their valiant efforts, Jacob curses them for their violent acts, for they have placed the Israelites in a prime position for a counterattack by fearful neighboring armies. In Genesis 49:5–7, Jacob declares:

Simeon and Levi are two of a kind—men of violence. O my soul, stay away from them. May I never be a party to their wicked plans. For in their anger they murdered men, and they crippled oxen just for sport. Cursed be their anger, for it is fierce; cursed be their wrath, for it is cruel. Therefore, I will scatter their descendants throughout the nation of Israel.

The moral of the story is that God doesn't need or want us to take matters into our own hands when we are wronged. Indeed, He declares that vengeance is His alone and that He will be the one to repay those who do evil against us (see Romans 12:19).

Do you leave vengeance to the Lord, or do you tend to take matters into your own hands? When someone offends you, do you turn the other cheek, as Jesus instructs (see Matthew 5:39; Luke 6:29), or do you try to offend that person right back? Can you let the situation go when you are wronged, or do you have to get even?

In order to live a pure life in a fallen world, we must choose to do as Christ would have us do. If someone offended a bride on her wedding day, the last thing she'd want to do is spoil the occasion even further by fighting back and creating a big scene. She'd look to her groom to step in and handle the situation quietly and peacefully. And that is exactly what we are to do every day of our lives. We must leave it to our heavenly Bridegroom to step in and achieve the victory on our behalf in every battle we face.

HOLDING HIS HAND

Have past events or abuses led me to want to seek vengeance, either consciously or subconsciously? If so, what has made me feel this way?

_____

_____

_____

If I took matters into my own hands and harmed this person, what would it ultimately accomplish? Would it fix anything or make the situation worse? How so?

_____

_____

_____

If I gave the battle over to the Lord and allowed Him to repay whoever has caused me pain, what would it accomplish? How would I feel about myself, God, and the other person as a result?

_____

_____

_____

Lord Jesus,

You are the ultimate big brother who seeks to protect Your vulnerable sisters. You are the heavenly Bridegroom who seeks to preserve the purity and honor of Your spiritual bride. Thank You that You are willing to seek revenge from my enemies so that I don't have to. I absolutely love that about You! Amen.

ISRAEL'S GOLDEN BOY

Daily reading: Exodus 31:18–32:35; 40

Key passage: Bring Aaron and his sons to the entrance of the Tabernacle, and wash them with water. Clothe Aaron with the holy garments and anoint him, setting him apart to serve me as a priest. Then bring his sons and dress them in their tunics. Anoint them as you did their father, so they may serve me as priests. With this anointing, Aaron's descendants are set apart for the priesthood forever, from generation to generation. (Exodus 40:12–15)

When I was ten years old, I was rearranging the furniture in my bedroom one day. When I tried to unplug my clock radio from behind the bed, I realized my short arms couldn't reach the outlet, so I tried to figure out a way around my predicament. I needed something long with which I could extend my reach, and I remembered a two-foot-long knife that my older brother, Bill, had purchased as a souvenir on a summer trip. It was an Arkansas Toothpick, and the metal blade was shiny and came to a sharp point at the tip. I figured it would be perfect for inserting between the wall outlet and the plastic handgrip on the electrical plug.

In my ignorance of how electricity is conducted through metal, I slid the knife behind my bed and tried to pry the plug from the outlet. As soon as the metal blade came in contact with the prongs of the plug, *Pow!* Sparks flew in every direction, and the blade was singed black on both edges. If the handle hadn't been made of wood, I'd have surely had an even more shocking experience!

Afraid I would be in big trouble if my brother or parents found out what I had done, I put the knife back into its leather case and returned it to my brother's desk drawer. A few weeks later, Bill yelled from his room, "Shannon Lynn, what happened to my knife?!!"

I panicked. *How did he know it was me?* Fearing he'd beat me to a pulp if he knew the truth, I tried to think of something fast. "What? What are you talking about?" I asked innocently.

"My knife! What happened to it?" Bill demanded.

"I don't know. What's wrong with it?" I asked, as if it wasn't incredibly obvious to the naked eye.

"It's ruined!"

"Oh, it's not ruined. You can still use it!" I replied with a half smile.

Growing impatient with me, Bill insisted, "You did something to it! What did you do?"

"Maybe somebody spilled something on it and it corroded!" I suggested.

He knew I was lying, dancing around his questions to avoid taking responsibility for what I had done. Once he showed the knife to our dad, my brother didn't have to beat me to a pulp. Dad did it for him, spanking me once for lying, another time for taking the knife without Bill's permission, and yet another time for endangering my life by sticking the knife into an electrical outlet. I should have left the knife alone in the first place or at least been more forthcoming in confessing my dangerous error.

In today's reading, we see Aaron doing something similar with his own brother. Moses has been up high on the mountain, receiving God's laws for how the Israelites are to worship the living God, while Aaron has been down low at the base of the mountain, leading the people in the sinful worship of a golden idol. Moses confronts Aaron with disbelief, asking, "What did the people do to you?... How did they ever make you bring such terrible sin upon them?" (Exodus 32:21).

In the verses that follow, we see Aaron begin to dance, pleading with Moses not to get upset (as if all the revelry and idolatry were no big deal). He scrambles to come up with a legitimate response, then resorts to, "You know how wicked these people are!" Translation: "It's all their fault, Moses. I had nothing to do with it" (as if he had no authority or control over them). Moses is still fuming, so Aaron digs a little deeper for an answer that will pacify his younger brother. "They didn't think you were coming back, so they told me to make some gods to lead them!" Sensing that Moses is still not satisfied, Aaron resorts to lying, insinuating that a miracle took place in Moses's absence. "I told them to bring their gold earrings, and when I threw them into the fire, this calf just popped out!" he exclaims.

Moses may have been born during the day, but certainly not the day before. He's been around the mountain enough times to know that Aaron wasn't being honest.

You might think this explosive episode marked the end of Aaron's career as a spiritual leader, wouldn't you? Actually, it was a distinct mark of the beginning. Just a few chapters later we see God instructing Moses to anoint and consecrate none other than Israel's golden boy, Aaron, as the head of the royal Levite priesthood. Hello? Had God forgotten Aaron's pathetic dance of deception? No, God hadn't forgotten. He had simply forgiven Aaron for his poor judgment. Perhaps God even used the golden calf incident to prepare Aaron for priestly service. As the Israelites came to him to make their confessions and offer sacrifices for their sins, surely Aaron would be able to sympathize with their weaknesses and offer them guidance on returning to a godly lifestyle.

Is there something in your past that you've assumed prevented you from spiritual advancement? If so, have you considered that perhaps God wants to redeem your mistake by using it to prepare you for ministry? It's a common theme throughout the Scriptures—God taking pathetic people and molding them into mighty ministers. Are you willing to let God mold you into one of His golden girls? If so, start by surrendering your excuses as to why God can't use you, and get ready to be utilized by our merciful Master.

HOLDING HIS HAND

Have I made excuses for my past sinful behaviors, not taking responsibility, or even blaming them on other people? If so, does this attitude do me any good?

_____

_____

_____

_____

What could God do through me if I bucked up, took responsibility for my own poor choices, and offered my broken life in service to Him?

_____

_____

_____

_____

How would it make me feel to watch God work through me to impact other people's lives to an even greater degree? Why?

_____

_____

_____

Awesome God,

The fact that You overlook even our most rebellious sins is such a testimony to Your mercy. Your lavish love for us leads us to want to shout Your praises from the mountaintops! Remove our miseries and show us how we can turn them into ministries that will lead others to respond to Your transforming grace as well. In Jesus' name. Amen.

R-E-S-P-E-C-T

Daily reading: 1 Samuel 2; 4

Key passage: Now the sons of Eli were scoundrels who had no respect for the Lord or for their duties as priests.... Now Eli was very old, but he was aware of what his sons were doing to the people of Israel. He knew, for instance, that his sons were seducing the young women who assisted at the entrance of the Tabernacle. Eli said to them, "I have been hearing reports from the people about the wicked things you are doing. Why do you keep sinning? You must stop, my sons!" (1 Samuel 2:12, 22–24)

I grew up attending church, and I never saw anyone in our congregation doing anything disrespectful or dishonorable to the Lord. However, when I went away to church camp the summer before my junior year in high school, I learned that not all Christians honor God with their behavior.

Although I knew Adam vaguely from school, I got to know him on a more personal level that summer at camp. He carried his Bible around and got in kids' faces, preaching the gospel. He sat at the dinner table creating all these similes about God's perfection, saying things such as, "God is like an untouched bank of snow… God is like a pristine sandy beach… God is like a freshly opened jar of marshmallow creme…" After several days of this, I began to believe that Adam was really on fire for the Lord.

When school resumed a few weeks later, I found that Adam and I were in the same journalism class right after lunch. He would often walk in from the school parking lot with bloodshot eyes, reeking of smoke and alcohol, unable to walk down the aisle without bumping into people. But then he'd sit down at his desk, pull his Bible out of his backpack, and tell teachers and other students they were going to hell if they judged him. I would cringe over his detestable behavior. He was the biggest hypocrite in our school, and I felt that he was making Christians look offensive to those who didn't know what Christians stood for.

But as frustrated as I was by my peer's behavior, I can only imagine how Eli must have felt over his own sons' detestable acts. As holy priests from the tribe of Levi, Eli's sons, Hophni and Phinehas, were supposed to fulfill one of the most honorable roles in service to God. As priests, they were entitled to a portion of the animals sacrificed to God. However, Hophni and Phinehas were not satisfied with their fair share. They wanted more, and against the offerers' wills they often stuck their forks into the sacrifices even before God had received them (or before the fat had burned off, which was a sign of His acceptance). Their actions exhibited a complete lack of reverence or respect. To add disrespect upon disrespect, the two men slept with the female assistants who served at the entrance of the tabernacle. Eli warned them that their actions would bring about God's judgment, but his disrespectful sons didn't heed his warning.

In 1 Samuel 4, we see the Israelite army being defeated twice, due to God's anger with what is being allowed to go on in the tabernacle. The Israelites, remembering that Joshua won the battle at Jericho as he carried the ark of the covenant before their army, attempt to repeat the miracle, but the miracle was not to be duplicated. The Israelites suffer thirty thousand casualties, their enemies capture the ark of the covenant, and Eli's two sons die in the battle.

But the retribution doesn't stop there. By his tolerance, Eli had shown that he was more committed to his sons than he was to God. When word reaches Eli that his sons died in battle and that the ark of the covenant had been captured, the obese priest falls out of his chair, breaks his neck, and dies. When this news reaches Eli's pregnant daughter-in-law, she goes into premature labor and dies as well. No wonder she named her baby Ichabod before she died (meaning "no glory"), for the glory had surely departed from Israel (see 1 Samuel 4:21–22).

As this story so powerfully illustrates, God may tolerate evil for a time in order to grant opportunity for repentance, but eventually such disrespect stirs His wrath. Paul warns us not to disrespect God when he writes, "Do not be deceived: God cannot be mocked. A man reaps what he sows. The one who sows to please his sinful nature, from that nature will reap destruction; the one who sows to please the Spirit, from the Spirit will reap eternal life" (Galatians 6:7–8, NIV). Hophni and Phinehas could have easily reaped the blessings of eternal life by respecting the leadership roles God had bestowed upon them. Instead, their disrespectful choices led them to destruction.

While we may not carry the religious responsibilities of these Jewish priests, we do wear the name tag "Christian." We are ambassadors of Christ (see 2 Corinthians 5:20), and we bear the responsibility of showing the world how a Christian embraces a lifestyle of sincere worship, fervent prayer, and faithful tithing. Do we lead others in these areas by example? Let's not embrace the "do as I say and not as I do" attitude that Hophni and Phinehas seemed to have. Instead, let's be a true reflection of our heavenly Bridegroom by always giving God the respect He demands and deserves.

HOLDING HIS HAND

Do I believe that Eli and his sons received their just punishment, or did God seem to be reacting a little too harshly? Why do I feel the way I do?

_____

_____

_____

Are these kinds of things still happening in some churches today? Dipping into the offering or withholding it altogether for personal gain? Falling into sexual temptations? How can I guard against these things becoming temptations in my own life?

_____

_____

_____

When I go to worship, pray, or give to God, what is the attitude of my heart? Am I truly doing it out of respectful obedience and gratitude, or am I just going through the motions of what is expected of me by others?

_____

_____

_____

Holy Lord,

We keep nothing hidden from You, for You see all things, even the motivations of our hearts. Cleanse us of any desires to withhold our earnest worship, prayers, and finances from You, for You are worthy of these things and so much more! Help us to show our respect and reverence for You in everything we do. In Jesus' name. Amen.

A WELL WOMAN

Daily reading: John 4:1–42

Key passage: Many Samaritans from the village believed in Jesus because the woman had said, "He told me everything I ever did!" When they came out to see him, they begged him to stay at their village. So he stayed for two days, long enough for many of them to hear his message and believe. Then they said to the woman, "Now we believe because we have heard him ourselves, not just because of what you told us. He is indeed the Savior of the world." (John 4:39–42)

*H*istorically, Jews and Samaritans made it a point never to mix or mingle with one another. However, in today's reading Jesus makes it a point to stop for a drink of water in the town of Samaria, where he strikes up a conversation with a Samaritan woman in spite of the cultural prohibition against a rabbi talking publicly with women. This is an unlikely encounter, set on an unlikely stage, yet we sense that Jesus' words and actions are intentional.[1]

The woman has a string of broken relationships behind her. She appears to be bound by chains of sexual immorality. After five husbands, she is living with a man she isn't married to, and her future likely promises continued dis-illusionment. That is, until Jesus comes into her life.

Jesus does not bother to question this woman as to why she is having an affair. He does not ask her what happened in her childhood that would jus-tify her immoral actions. He does not ask her what pain she is trying to escape through her inappropriate relationships. Jesus knows it would do no good to allow her an opportunity to blame her sin on external factors, as is sometimes the response in today's society to dysfunctional behaviors.

No, Jesus masterfully cuts to the chase. He reveals to her that the place where we worship God isn't nearly as important as the attitude with which we worship Him. He recognizes her spiritual curiosity, knowing she is thirsty for fulfillment. He knows she has been looking for love but settling for sex—drinking stagnant water when only He could quench the overwhelming thirst in her spirit. He offers her a drink of living water so her very soul would know complete satisfaction for the first time.

And what is this woman's response to Jesus' revelations about her? She goes running back to her hometown to tell everyone about her spiritually intimate encounter with a man who might very well be the Messiah they've been waiting for. While most townspeople would never believe the testimony of a woman of such ill repute, the difference in her countenance is so unde-niable that they are open to discovering more about this Jesus. They invite Him to stay, and through their own personal encounter with Christ, they also became faithful followers. Her testimony started a spark in the town of Samaria, and Jesus fanned that spark into a flame.

The good news for us is that Jesus Christ is the same "yesterday, today, and forever" (Hebrews 13:8). He still stands at the well, awaiting broken women to approach Him with parched lips and dry throats, desperate for something to satisfy our weary souls. My sister, have you ever wondered what it would be like to have the thirst of your soul quenched in such a way that you would never again thirst for unhealthy relationships? In your attempts to feel loved, are you aware that Jesus Christ longs to be the Lover of your soul? If inappropriate relationships have been an issue in your life, are you aware there is a new life waiting for you that is free from such stresses, worries, dangers, and emotional roller-coaster rides? Your God longs to see you at peace in your relationship with Him; He longs to fill you with the fruit of His Spirit—"love, joy, peace, patience, kindness, goodness, faithfulness, gentleness, and self-control" (Galatians 5:22–23).

If you have had a tendency to spell love with the wrong three letters (M-E-N rather than G-O-D), know that Christ wants to transform you from a woman at the well into a well woman. He wants to show you where satisfaction can be found. Just as the Samaritan woman experienced centuries ago, a face-to-face encounter with Jesus Christ can heal your wounds and satisfy your thirst for a genuinely fulfilling relationship. It can bring years of dysfunctional patterns to a close and help you live a life of virtue. Once you taste the living water that only Christ can offer, you'll never go back to stagnant water again!

HOLDING HIS HAND

Do you attract dysfunctional relationships? Does the word *codependent* describe you at all? Do you look to men for a sense of identity and security? If so, why?

_____

_____

_____

_____

_____

Do you see yourself as a well woman (someone who knows that satisfaction is only found in Jesus) rather than a woman at the well (someone who looks for love in the wrong places)? If so, why? If not, what would it take for you to move in that direction?

_____

_____

_____

_____

_____

If Jesus has already changed your life in such a way, do you have a tendency to hide your past from others, or are you willing to unashamedly let your light shine so that others will know of Christ's transforming power?

_____

_____

_____

_____

_____

Dearest Jesus,

Thank You for breaking all the traditions of Your culture to demonstrate to us how much You long to see our spiritual thirst completely quenched. Forgive us for all the ways we have looked for love in the wrong places, and show us how to live every day as well women! Amen.

A SELFISH CLIMB UP THE CORPORATE LADDER

Daily reading: 2 Kings 11; James 3:13–18

Key passage: If you are bitterly jealous and there is selfish ambition in your hearts, don't brag about being wise. That is the worst kind of lie. For jealousy and selfishness are not God's kind of wisdom. Such things are earthly, unspiritual, and motivated by the Devil. For wherever there is jealousy and selfish ambition, there you will find disorder and every kind of evil. (James 3:14–16)

---

*A*lthough you may never have heard of Athaliah, she's an incredibly memorable biblical character once you know her story. She was Jezebel's daughter (we'll read more about the controlling Jezebel soon), and her violent quest for power and control proves that she learned a few things from her mama before she left home.

Upon discovering that her son, the reigning king, is dead, Athaliah doesn't waste time dressing in black and mourning her loss at his grave side. Instead, she immediately kills all other heirs to the throne so that she will be elevated to power as queen. As shocking as it may seem, Athaliah didn't get someone else do her dirty work for her. The Bible says Athaliah herself "set out to destroy the rest of the royal family" (2 Kings 11:1). I've heard of mothers killing their own children by reason of insanity, but never out of a quest for power. I can't imagine a more hardhearted woman.

Fortunately, God uses another woman to hide one remaining infant heir to the throne, who after six years would emerge from hiding to take his rightful place as the nation's seven-year-old king. At this point, Athaliah also takes her rightful place in the palace—at the hands of the guards who slay her with a sword, perhaps the method she used to slay her own family members years before.

The first few times I read about Athaliah, I made no personal connection between her life and mine. But then I heard my dear friend Liz Curtis Higgs speak about some of the "really bad girls of the Bible" and what she had in common with them (since many of us identify far more closely with the bad girls than the good girls). Liz recalled a season of her life when she, like Athaliah, had subconsciously made her family take a backseat to her career ambitions. Her words reminded me that my ministry as a mother and wife should always be more important than my ministry to anyone else. How many times have I chosen to spend precious moments writing on my laptop instead of loving on my kids and husband? It's not that we need to be in our families' faces 24/7 to show our love, but we sometimes allow our selfish ambitions to rob our children and husbands of the quality time they need with us.

I can recall the emptiness I felt when my father always seemed to have "too much to do" in his workshop to spend any quality time with our family. He only came in for dinner, which my mom served him in his recliner in front of the television. Then it was back out to the shop until way past our bedtime. This painful memory once came flooding back into my mind while I was on a writing retreat, hoping to get ahead on some project. Along with the memory came a sobering thought: *What's the difference between a welding project and a writing project in a kid's mind? Should I expect my children to have more grace for my writing retreats than I had for my dad's late-night work projects? Just because my busyness is all in the name of ministry, does that make my absence any easier on my family?*

I prayed about where I stood with my commitments to my publisher and realized that my time away was really optional. Then I called my husband and told him I was cutting my trip in half, coming home two days early. "Is everything okay?" he asked. I told him it would be once I was back home where I belonged.

Have there been seasons in your life when you have allowed your balance between marriage, motherhood, ministry, and/or career to get out of sync? While we all have to make sacrifices at times to accomplish necessary tasks, have you chosen to sacrifice too much time with your family in order to climb the corporate ladder? Let us remember the old saying:

> No one on their deathbed is likely to say, "I wish I had spent more time at the office!"

Let's spend more time focusing quality time and attention on those who are truly most important to us—our God and the family and friends He has blessed us with.

HOLDING HIS HAND

Are my ambitions in alignment with God's desires for my life, or do I tend to selfishly want more? What makes me feel the way I do?

_____

_____

_____

Where do I believe my identity and significance come from? Do I feel a sense of personal fulfillment simply by being a child of God, or do I need prestige and promotion to feel as if I am somebody?

_____

_____

_____

How can I protect myself and my ambitions from becoming selfish? How can I tell when I'm expecting others to sacrifice too much so I can accomplish my own goals? Where do I draw the line?

_____

_____

_____

Lord God,

So often we feel the need to do more and become more so we can impress others or feel better about ourselves. But nothing will ever satisfy our quest for power and honor aside from simply realizing who we are in Christ. Remind us that we are Your chosen elect, and help us fully embrace the roles You've given us as Your beloved bride. Amen.

EXPECTING THE
EXTRAORDINARY

Daily reading: 1 Kings 19:1–18

Key passage: Elijah was afraid and fled for his life. He went to Beersheba, a town in Judah, and he left his servant there. Then he went on alone into the desert, traveling all day. He sat down under a solitary broom tree and prayed that he might die. "I have had enough, LORD," he said. "Take my life, for I am no better than my ancestors." (1 Kings 19:3–4)

ave you ever met a bold, daring, brave, heroic…coward? That's the impression we get of Elijah, post Mount Carmel. Earlier, this man had boldly declared the sovereignty of God, tested the wicked King Ahab with a three-year drought, called down both fire and rain from heaven, and slain 450 prophets of Baal. Elijah probably wished his story ended there, for in this chapter, we see quite a different prophet, one running out of town with his proverbial tail between his legs. What set his heart ablaze with fear? One woman.

Of course, Jezebel was no ordinary woman. She was a queen who was infamous for her evil ways (we'll talk more about her tomorrow). Even her husband, King Ahab, seemed to fear her. When Ahab tells his wife about the defeat and death of the 450 prophets of Baal, he credits Elijah, not God. Jezebel is enraged with the prophet and insists she's going to have Elijah for lunch, not as a guest, but as the entrée.

So what does Elijah do, having already stood firm in his faith before kings and hundreds of false prophets? He turns and runs, begging God to take his life before Jezebel does. Hello? Elijah? Don't you remember who you are? Or whose you are? You are the chosen prophet of the almighty God! Yet you run away from a single wicked woman?

What was going through Elijah's mind as he ran away? While we can only speculate, I believe 1 Kings 19:4–10 gives us pretty good clues. First, God gives him rest under the shade of a tree, then nourishment, then more rest and more nourishment. It's a great prescription for anyone who is feeling tired, overwhelmed, stressed, and depressed—to rest in the Lord's presence and tend to your body's basic needs.

Once Elijah is rested and fed, God's Spirit leads him on a forty-day trek to Mount Sinai (where God revealed Himself to Moses). On that mountain, Elijah witnesses a terrible windstorm, expecting God to be in it, but He isn't. Then comes a great earthquake, but God isn't in that either. A great fire appears, but God's still not there. Finally, Elijah hears a gentle whisper and recognizes it as the Lord's voice (see verses 11–13).

What is the correlation between the scene of God sending down fire from heaven one minute and the next scene of Him revealing Himself in a gentle whisper? Elijah had seen God's power over and over in the extraordinary, but God wanted Elijah to understand that He's in the ordinary as well. Perhaps Elijah had expected Jezebel to hear about the happenings at Mount Carmel and to repent of her wicked ways. Maybe Elijah had expected she'd spontaneously combust when all the prophets of Baal were killed. He was looking for God to intervene in an extraordinary way, but that wasn't God's plan in that situation. When God didn't live up to Elijah's expectations, the prophet slipped into a deep, crippling fear and an almost suicidal depression. Rather than simply adjusting his expectations and continuing to trust in God, Elijah panicked and ran. Even God's boldest and best can cower when God doesn't do as they expect.

What about you? Are there circumstances in your life that cause you to wonder where God is and why He's not doing what you expect of Him? Perhaps you need to adjust your expectations. God may be demonstrating His powers through the ordinary rather than through some extraordinary display. Can you accept that His ways are higher than your ways, even if they don't measure up to your expectations?

It's not realistic to expect God to work in extraordinary ways every single day of our lives. He wants us to have more faith in Him than that. We can't live from one mountaintop experience to the next, assuming God isn't there or isn't working unless we're feeling a spiritual high.

No matter how good or how bad things are going, God never leaves us or forsakes us. With this knowledge firmly planted in your heart and mind, you never have to fear. You never need to run away to find protection. You never have to sink into a state of depression, because God is often at work behind the scenes, working through ordinary means in order to exceed your expectations. After all, our God isn't just the Lord of the mountaintops, but He's Lord of the valleys as well.

HOLDING HIS HAND

Do I tend to assume that God only works in the extraordinary, not the ordinary, moments of life? Why or why not?

_____

_____

_____

Do I get fearful or depressed whenever I can't recognize how God is working in a situation? If so, what does this fear or depression say about my faith in God?

_____

_____

_____

Rather than get depressed, how can I face my fears with confidence that God is in control when I am feeling out-of-control?

_____

_____

_____

Most awesome Lord,

*Who are we to assume that You should do things our way?
Yet we often grow fearful and depressed when You aren't
working the way we expect You to. Forgive us for our lack of
faith in Your mysterious ways. Remind us that You are always
working things for our good, not just in extraordinary ways,
but in ordinary ways as well. In Jesus' name. Amen.*

THE QUEEN OF CONTROL

Daily reading: 1 Kings 21; 2 Kings 9

Key passage: The LORD has also told me that the dogs of Jezreel will eat the body of your wife, Jezebel, at the city wall. The members of your family who die in the city will be eaten by dogs, and those who die in the field will be eaten by vultures."

No one else so completely sold himself to what was evil in the LORD's sight as did Ahab, for his wife, Jezebel, influenced him. (1 Kings 21:23–25)

---

*I*n my late teens and early twenties, I had an unusual occupation that left a lasting impression on me. I grew up wanting to be a medical pathologist (like Jack Klugman on the television show *Quincy*). But since I couldn't afford medical school, I settled for going to mortuary college and becoming an embalmer and funeral director instead. During the four years that I worked in the mortuary business, I attended countless funerals, some tragically sad, some lighthearted and celebratory, and others somewhere in between.

As a result of that work, I frequently think about the details of my own funeral. I wonder who will attend, what songs will be played, what will be said, and where I'll be buried. I've visited neighboring cemeteries, letting my family know my wishes. While I'm not even forty years old yet, I've also considered having one of those prearranged funeral plans. Sometimes my family thinks I'm crazy or morbid, but I tell them, "You'll thank me come that time!" I vividly remember the confusion and chaos in families who had no prior arrangements for their lost loved one, as well as the sense of peace demonstrated by the families that did.

There've been times when I have read the story of Jezebel and wondered if she ever thought about her own funeral and burial wishes. If so, I'm sure her plans would never have included being eaten by dogs and scattered "like dung on the field of Jezreel, so that no one will be able to recognize her" (2 Kings 9:37). And what would those who survived Jezebel say about her? What would she be remembered for? According to what the Bible tells us about her life, she was infamous for having led her husband, King Ahab, into Baal worship (see 1 Kings 16:31). She attempted to kill off the prophets of God (see 1 Kings 18:4), so I'm not sure anyone who escaped her treachery would have offered a very eloquent eulogy. As we discussed yesterday, she wanted Elijah dead as well, so he may have wanted to be a pallbearer just so he could throw the first shovel of dirt on her wrapped corpse (or roll the stone in front of the tomb, as was the custom in that day).

No wonder Jezebel is remembered as the queen of heartless manipulation and control. Not only do we see this in her dealings with Elijah and the prophets of God but also in how she treated Naboth, who refused to sell his family's land to Ahab. When her husband gets upset over this, Jezebel arrogantly assumes that whatever the king wants, the king should get. She creates an elaborate plan to steal the property from the rightful owner, sending forged letters to the elders of the community sealed with Ahab's seal, inviting them to a special assembly. There, two accusers point the finger at Naboth and falsely claim that he blasphemed both God and Ahab. As a result, Naboth is stoned to death, and Jezebel has his sons killed as well in order to eliminate all possible heirs of the property (see 2 Kings 9:26). The land now belongs to the king's family, along with even more bloodguilt.

Later, Jehu is anointed king and given the charge of destroying all of Ahab's family (particularly Jezebel) because of their wickedness and idolatry. In this way, the blood of God's prophets whom Jezebel killed could be avenged. Jehu rides into town after killing Jehoram (who had embraced the idolatry that Jezebel introduced into the kingdom). His mission is to kill Jezebel next. Rather than humble herself and plead for mercy, Jezebel spews out one last insult, shouting to Jehu, "You are just like Zimri, who murdered his master" (2 Kings 9:31), because of his betrayal.

Jezebel's moment of judgment finally arrives. When Jehu asks for help in killing her, her own eunuchs push Jezebel out the window. As if her body splattering on the ground isn't cruel enough punishment, Jehu proceeds to ride his horse right over her body and into his new palace. Later, Jehu decides that Jezebel should be buried properly since she is the daughter of a king, but it's too late for a proper burial. The dogs have helped themselves to her remains, fulfilling the prophecy spoken against her that "dogs will eat Ahab's wife, Jezebel, at the plot of land in Jezreel, and no one will bury her" (2 Kings 9:10).

While no one wants to be identified with Jezebel, we, too, sometimes try to manipulate situations and control people in order to get our way. When our kids don't do exactly as we ask, we often resort to manipulative control (rather than proper discipline) to get them to comply. When our husbands don't give us what we want, when we want it, we can act less like Mrs. Right and more like Mrs. *Always* Right, attempting to exert control over them. One woman confessed to me, "I can get my husband to do just about anything I want. All I have to do is cross my legs and stop cooking!" Or perhaps we attempt to keep co-workers under our thumbs, insisting that things be done "my way or the highway." The Jezebel spirit is still alive and well in many homes and offices today.

If you want to live out your righteousness, recognize and repent of any Jezebel spirit that is living in you. Instead of resorting to manipulation and control, a better, more effective strategy would be to *inspire* cooperation rather than *require* it. Each of us is a small part of a larger team. As we show proper respect and appreciation toward all our valuable teammates, we will surely be forever remembered, not as queens of control, but as beloved women of God.

HOLDING HIS HAND

Have I ever been accused of being manipulative or controlling? If so, was there any truth to the claim? How did I respond?

_____

_____

_____

Do I recognize a Jezebel spirit in myself? If so, in what ways does this spirit of control manifest itself in my life?

_____

_____

_____

How do I want to be remembered once I am no longer walking this earth? What things in my life may need to change in order to be remembered that way?

_____

_____

_____

Dearest Lord,

From Eve's time in the garden, through Jezebel's reign, right to today, the spirit of control often permeates women's lives and ruins our testimonies. We want others to remember us as women of character and influence, not as women of control and manipulation. We invite You to search our hearts, God, and show us if there are any ways in us that need to change. Amen.

CASTING PEARLS
BEFORE SWINE

Daily reading: Judges 13:1–5; 14:1–16:31

Key passage: Then Delilah pouted, "How can you say you love me when you don't confide in me? You've made fun of me three times now, and you still haven't told me what makes you so strong!" So day after day she nagged him until he couldn't stand it any longer.

Finally, Samson told her his secret. "My hair has never been cut," he confessed, "for I was dedicated to God as a Nazirite from birth. If my head were shaved, my strength would leave me, and I would become as weak as anyone else." (Judges 16:15–17)

While Samson will be forever known for his tremendous strength, he also went down in the history books as someone with a tremendous weakness, especially for Philistine women. In fact, Samson's story begins and ends with his falling prey to a woman's manipulations. His lust leads to the death of many and eventually leads to his own death as well. Between the beginning and the end of Samson's life, however, we see the Lord strengthening him in supernatural ways, all for His glory.

The story begins with Samson's parents dedicating him to God as a Nazirite, and as such he's forbidden to drink wine, come in contact with a corpse, or cut his hair. As an Israelite, Samson is also expected to refrain from intermarrying. However, Samson sets his eyes on a Philistine woman and insists on marrying her.

At a wedding preparation feast, Samson banters back and forth with thirty guests and tosses out a riddle, along with a wager. If the guests can solve the riddle, they each get a set of clothes. If not, they each award him with a set of clothes. Samson stands the chance of becoming the best-dressed guy in town, but instead he gives in to his wife's manipulative weeklong pouting party. She leaks the answer, the guests solve the riddle, and Samson has to pay up. Because the guests cheated Samson by pressing his wife for the answer, Samson feels justified in killing thirty men from the Philistine town of Ashkelon and stripping them of their garments in order to pay his debt.

Furious about the outcome of the bet, Samson temporarily abandons his new bride. When he later returns for her, he discovers that her father has already given her in marriage to his best man. Now Samson's even more furious. He retaliates against his father-in-law's people by setting their crops, vineyards, and olive groves ablaze with the help of three hundred foxes. Naturally, the Philistines don't take too kindly to his actions. They burn Samson's bride and father-in-law as payback. Samson retaliates once again by killing many more, and the Philistines soon come knocking on Israel's door, looking for Samson.

The Israelites cower, and in an attempt to keep peace, they hand Samson over to the Philistines, who bind him with new ropes. Of course, Samson breaks those new ropes as if they were licorice sticks, then takes the jawbone of a donkey and kills thousands of Philistines with it. When the Lord gives him twenty years of leadership as Israel's judge, it seems like Samson has learned his lesson.

However, another pretty face eventually enters the picture, and Samson goes gaga over a girl once again. Delilah, a prostitute, proves to be more temptation than Samson can withstand, and he allows himself to be manipulated again. For eleven hundred shekels of silver (over thirty-six times the price of one slave) from each Philistine leader, Delilah agrees to find out the secret of his strength. When Samson finally tells her that his uncut hair is the secret of his strength, she cuts it when he's asleep and lets in the Philistines so they can capture and bind him. Imprisoned, blinded, and humiliated, Samson is held captive long enough for his hair to grow back. Then comes the day of reckoning, when Samson pushes the pillars of the temple from their bases, killing the dignitaries inside, thousands of spectators, and himself in the process.

Although Samson rebelled against God at times, God actually used his rebellion to put him in position to be a major thorn in the side of the Philistines. Regardless of Samson's spiritual shortcomings, the Spirit of the Lord continually came upon him to perform great feats:

- "At that moment *the Spirit of the LORD powerfully took control of him*, and he ripped the lion's jaws apart with his bare hands. He did it as easily as if it were a young goat" (Judges 14:6).

- "Then *the Spirit of the LORD powerfully took control of him*. He went down to the town of Ashkelon, killed thirty men, took their belongings, and gave their clothing to the men who had answered his riddle" (Judges 14:19).

- "As Samson arrived at Lehi, the Philistines came shouting in triumph. But *the Spirit of the LORD powerfully took control of Samson*, and he snapped the ropes on his arms as if they were burnt strands of flax, and they fell from his wrists. Then he picked up a donkey's jawbone that was lying on the ground and killed a thousand Philistines with it" (Judges 15:14–15).

- "Then Samson prayed to the LORD, 'Sovereign LORD, remember me again. *O God, please strengthen me one more time* so that I may pay back the Philistines for the loss of my eyes'" (Judges 16:28).

What a powerful demonstration that God can even use our weaknesses to bring about His sovereign will.

We can only imagine how much greater and stronger Samson would have been had he not been so prone to casting his pearls (precious secrets) before swine (ill-intentioned women). No doubt God can also use our weaknesses to bring about His sovereign will, but are there times when we, like Samson, unnecessarily cast our pearls before swine? For example, do we lack discernment in what information we divulge to other people? Do we sometimes confess our weaknesses to those who may seek to take advantage of them? I frequently tell women, "Don't tell a guy where you keep your goat, or else he's going to get it!" We don't have to foolishly advertise what our weaknesses are. We just need to rest assured that God can (and will) use not only our strengths but also our weaknesses for His ultimate glory.

HOLDING HIS HAND

Jesus said, "Don't give what is holy to unholy people. Don't give pearls to swine! They will trample the pearls, then turn and attack you" (Matthew 7:6). What does this passage mean to me?

_____

_____

_____

Have I ever been accused of having "loose lips," divulging too much information that could bring harm to myself or to a trusting confidant? If so, what caused me to do this?

_____

_____

_____

_____

Have there been situations where God worked in spite of my weaknesses? If so, what might God have been doing through the situation?

_____

_____

_____

> *Precious Lord,*
>
> *Thank You for being the kind of God who can accomplish Your will even through our weaknesses. It's great to realize that our sinfulness doesn't negate Your sovereignty. Continue to do Your will in us, through us, and in spite of us when necessary. Amen.*

CAUGHT IN THE ACT

Daily reading: John 8:1–11

Key passage: They were trying to trap him into saying something they could use against him, but Jesus stooped down and wrote in the dust with his finger. They kept demanding an answer, so he stood up again and said, "All right, stone her. But let those who have never sinned throw the first stones!" (John 8:6–7)

*I*magine it's early in the morning and you are in the temple with a growing crowd of people, mesmerized by the wisdom and authority Jesus displays as He's teaching. Suddenly, several religious leaders barge in to the meeting and fling a scantily clad woman in Jesus' direction, obviously against her will. She frantically tries to cover herself as best she can. Her hair hangs in front of her face, partially covering it, but not so much that you can't see her intense anger, fear, and humiliation. Rather than question the woman, the Pharisees question Jesus. "Teacher…this woman was caught in the very act of adultery. The law of Moses says to stone her. What do you say?" (John 8:4–5).

You get a knot in your stomach, suspecting that this is a Catch-22 situation, some sort of test the Pharisees have devised out of hatred and envy of

Jesus. If Jesus says the woman shouldn't be stoned, the legalistic Pharisees will surely attempt to charge Him with disregarding the law, which could result in Jesus' death.[1] If Jesus says she should be stoned, He'll lose the reputation He's built as a man of compassion, and the woman will be put to death. Either way, someone loses big time.

But rather than respond, Jesus silently stoops down and begins scribbling in the dirt. You push through the crowd and lean in close to make out what He's writing, but it's impossible to decipher. You begin to speculate. *Could He be listing the sins of all the Pharisees present? Or perhaps listing the names of the Pharisees who had also slept with this same woman, or another prostitute perhaps? Is He just doodling, giving them time to think about what they are doing?*

The Pharisees won't drop it. They keep pressing Jesus for an answer to their question. Jesus stands up, looks them in the face, and says, "All right, stone her" (verse 7). *Uh-oh!* you are thinking. *Things are about to get violent.* You look at the Pharisees, with their holier-than-thou looks on their faces, and at the menacing stones in their hands. You look at the woman cowering down in the dirt, trembling, expecting to feel the pain of rocks pelting her body any second. However, Jesus suddenly continues, "But let those who have never sinned throw the first stones" (verse 7). Then He stoops down again and scribbles some more.

The Pharisees' mouths fall open at the audacity of Jesus to say such a thing to them. They look around at one another, bewildered and at a complete loss as to what to say in response. Moments later, their mouths close and their eyes fall to the ground, followed by the bowing of their heads. Their hands open, and you hear rocks fall to the ground, one by one. The woman hears the sounds too. She looks up to see what's happening, and she is stunned and overwhelmed with relief to see that the rocks are not being hurled in her direction. Eventually, the older Pharisees leave (I wonder, were they convicted or ashamed?), followed by the younger ones, until all the woman's accusers are gone. Jesus then asks her, "Where are your accusers? Didn't even one of them condemn you?" (verse 10).

The woman speaks for the first time. "No, Lord" (verse 11) was all she said, a new look of humility and hope in her eyes.

Jesus takes her by the hand, lifts her from the ground, smiles at her, and declares, "I don't either. You are free to go, but leave your sin here with me."

While I've taken a few creative liberties with the biblical story, the message is still the same. Even when we are in the very act of sin, our omnipotent (is everywhere) and omniscient (sees everything) God has a heart of compassion toward us. Before we even recognize our own transgressions, Jesus is beckoning us to turn from our sin and run into His arms. Only one question needs to be answered:

> *Will we leave our sin behind, respond to His transforming grace, and live forever free of guilt and condemnation?*

Like the woman caught in adultery, let us recognize the unconditional love and mercy of our heavenly Bridegroom, then be inspired to go and sin no more.

HOLDING HIS HAND

Has God ever "caught me in the act" of sin? If so, how did this make me feel?

_____

_____

_____

If Jesus responded in such a compassionate way toward this woman caught in the act of adultery, how do I suppose He responds to my sin? Why?

_____

_____

_____

What did Jesus mean when He told the woman to "go and sin no more"? Is this advice that I have accepted from Jesus as well? Why or why not?

_____

_____

_____

Lord Jesus,

We all know what it feels like to be undeniably guilty. What we don't know is how You can show such compassion, mercy, and love toward rebels like us. When we sin, please give us repentant hearts, free us from any fear of our accusers, and inspire us to run unashamedly into Your arms of comfort and protection. Amen.

DAVID'S UNTHINKABLE DEEDS

Daily reading: 2 Samuel 11:1–12:25

Key passage: Then Nathan said to David, "You are that man! The LORD, the God of Israel, says, 'I anointed you king of Israel and saved you from the power of Saul. I gave you his house and his wives and the kingdoms of Israel and Judah. And if that had not been enough, I would have given you much, much more. Why, then, have you despised the word of the LORD and done this horrible deed? For you have murdered Uriah and stolen his wife. From this time on, the sword will be a constant threat to your family, because you have despised me by taking Uriah's wife to be your own.'" (2 Samuel 12:7–10)

*M*any descriptive words come to mind when we think of David— shepherd boy, giant slayer, anointed king, eloquent psalmist… But in today's reading, we see that he is also capable of being a slacker…a Peeping Tom…an adulterer…a manipulator…and a murderer. How difficult to imagine that the "man after [God's] own heart" (1 Samuel 13:14) could harden his heart to the point that he would do these unthinkable deeds!

The story begins with an almost unnoticeable tidbit of information—that it's springtime, when kings go off to battle, yet David is sending his troops to war while he is on spring vacation at the palace. Had he been tending to business, surely what is about to happen would not have happened. While his soldiers are out on the front lines of battle, hurling spears at their enemies, David is waking up from a late-afternoon catnap and taking a leisurely stroll on his rooftop.

From there he sees a bathing beauty, Bathsheba, and his heart and hormones race. He inquires as to who she is and finds out that she is the wife of one of his soldiers, Uriah. That information alone should have been enough to shoo any lustful thoughts from his mind, but alas, David uses his royal power to draw Uriah's wife into his private chambers, where he commits adultery with her.

Then the announcement comes. Bathsheba is pregnant with David's child. So what does David do? He goes into manipulation mode. First, he tells her husband, Uriah, to take a break from the battle and encourages him to go home, where David assumes he'll sleep with his wife. But Uriah proves to have far more integrity than David, refusing to go home and eat, drink, and sleep with his wife when his fellow soldiers are sleeping without supper in the open fields. So David gets the man drunk, thinking surely he'll let down his guard and sleep with his wife. But even under the influence of alcohol, Uriah has more of a conscience than David.

Desperate times call for desperate measures, and David is definitely desperate at this point. He sends Uriah back into battle, carrying a message to Joab, the commander of the army, to put Uriah in the front lines so he'll be killed. After two failed attempts, David finally "solves" his problem, at least the problem of what the neighbors would think. But David seems unconcerned at this point about what God thinks.

After Bathsheba's time of mourning, David brings her into the palace and makes her his wife. Shortly afterward the prophet Nathan arrives on the scene to share a parable with the king that will expose his guilt and bring David to repentance. While we can only imagine the overwhelming anger the Lord must have felt over David's unthinkable deeds, note what Nathan says to this adulterous, murderous king. When David confesses, "I have sinned against the LORD," Nathan responds, "Yes, but the LORD *has forgiven you*" (2 Samuel 12:13). The prophet doesn't say the Lord *will* forgive you, but rather, the Lord *has* [already] forgiven you. What mercy God displays toward David!

Not to say that all consequences are removed, for David suffers the loss of his newborn child. However, he does not suffer the loss of God's lavish love, nor his position of leadership over the kingdom of Israel, nor the honor of being the bloodline through which the Messiah would be born. Even more amazing, David and Bathsheba are together in the lineage of Christ through their son Solomon (see Matthew 1:3–6). In fact, God remembers David for his honorable position rather than his dishonorable acts, as seen throughout the New Testament, written long after David's fall from grace:

- "Praise the Lord, the God of Israel, because he has visited his people and redeemed them. He has sent us a mighty Savior from the *royal line of his servant David,* just as he promised through his holy prophets long ago" (Luke 1:68–70).
- "For the Scriptures clearly state that the Messiah will be born of *the royal line of David,* in Bethlehem, the village where King David was born" (John 7:42).
- "God removed [Saul] from the kingship and replaced him with David, a man about whom God said, 'David son of Jesse is *a man after my own heart,* for he will do everything I want him to'" (Acts 13:22).
- "It is the Good News about his Son, Jesus, who came as a man, *born into King David's royal family line*" (Romans 1:3).

So why would God bestow such honor and favor on a man who had committed such heinous acts? I believe it is because of David's response to

God's conviction. Although it took awhile for the magnitude of his sin to sink in, David humbly conceded to whatever punishment God saw fit to lay on him, because he knew that what he had done was wrong.

Similarly, most of us have committed some misdeed that we know is far from acceptable to God. We wonder in hindsight, *How could I have done that? And how could God possibly have forgiven me for it?* Realize that although our sin is not acceptable to God, we as divinely redeemed humans are always acceptable to Him. All our imperfections have been blotted out by the perfect blood of Christ, and all that God sees when He gazes upon us is the radiance of His beautiful bride, completely forgiven and clothed in white.

HOLDING HIS HAND

Do I feel that David received more or less of a punishment than he deserved for his misdeeds? Why do I feel the way I do?

_____

_____

_____

Do I believe that I have the favor of the Lord, in spite of my past sinful misdeeds? Why or why not?

_____

_____

_____

Do I live each day knowing that I am a woman after God's own heart? If so, how does it affect my life? If not, what is holding me back from feeling this way?

_____

_____

_____

Most holy God,

So often we allow our sin to separate us from You, not because of Your lack of mercy, but because of our lack of faith in Your mercy. Thank You for showing us through David's life that You quickly forgive sin when we have repentant hearts. Help us to believe wholeheartedly that Christ's sacrificial death clothed us completely in white and that we are radiantly pure in Your eyes. In our heavenly Bridegroom's holy name. Amen.

THE ROOT OF ALL EVIL

Daily reading: Matthew 26:1–5, 14–30, 36–56; 27:1–10; John 12:1–8; 1
Timothy 6:3–10

Key passage: Then Judas Iscariot, one of the twelve disciples, went to the
leading priests and asked, "How much will you pay me to betray Jesus to
you?" And they gave him thirty pieces of silver. From that time on, Judas
began looking for the right time and place to betray Jesus. (Matthew
26:14–16)

Scripture tells us that the "love of money is at the root of all kinds of
evil" (1 Timothy 6:10). I can think of no better example of this than
Judas Iscariot. While we may wonder what caused him to betray Jesus the
way he did, a closer look at several verses reveals that his intense financial
greed may have motivated his mission.

We see our first glimpse into Judas' questionable character as Mary
anoints Jesus' feet with perfume in order to prepare Him for burial. She seems
to correctly sense that the time is coming when she will no longer have her
Master with her, and she wants to demonstrate her lavish love for Him. The
perfume she uses is very costly, worth approximately three hundred denarii
(nearly a year's wages), and may be part, if not all, of her dowry.[1]

But as the group treasurer, Judas complains that Mary's sacrifice is wasteful. "It could have been sold and the money given to the poor!" he cries. But Judas cares for the poor about as much as a buffalo cares for a bubble bath. He apparently wants to pad the treasury so that he can have a larger reserve from which to pad his own pocket, as he has done previously (see John 12:6).

Jesus rebukes Judas, insisting that what he calls "wasteful" is both appropriate and appreciated. "You will always have the poor among you," Jesus says in verse 8, reminding Judas that if he's really concerned for the poor, he'll continue to have plenty of opportunities to help them after Jesus is gone (not that Judas intends to do this!).

Perhaps Jesus' public and humiliating words stung Judas' ego, creating a desire for revenge. Or maybe Judas began to question whether Jesus was really the Messiah since He often acted more like a pauper than a prince, more like a slave than a savior. But I suspect Judas was motivated by the money he knew he could get by offering Jesus into the hands of the leading priests.

Regardless of his reasons, Judas chooses to sell out his Lord for thirty pieces of silver, the price of a common slave. Yet he still dines with Jesus in the Upper Room, denying that he is about to betray Him. What's worse is the way he chooses to betray Jesus—with a kiss on the cheek, which was a symbol of friendship.

Even though Jesus has known of Judas' intentions from the beginning, I find it astounding that His reply to Judas' kiss is, "*My friend,* go ahead and do what you have come for" (Matthew 26:50). If I had been in Jesus' sandals at that moment, I can think of a whole list of names I might have called Judas—Traitor! Liar! Backstabber!—but Jesus calls him "friend." Even as He is being betrayed, Jesus intentionally demonstrates His love for sinners.

Perhaps the look of love and compassion in Jesus' eyes is what prompts Judas to return to the Pharisees and confess, "I have sinned...for I have betrayed an innocent man" (Matthew 27:4). But the Pharisees couldn't care less about Judas' error in judgment. They've got their man, and they are not about to give Him up. Overwhelmed with remorse, Judas throws the money at them and runs away, finding a noose around his neck less painful to bear than his guilty conscience.

I've often wondered if Judas didn't get a raw deal, in that someone had to step forward as the betrayer who would fulfill all the prophecies surrounding Jesus' death. Wasn't he really just God's puppet? But I've come to realize that Judas, like all of us, had free will. He could have said no, he would not betray his Lord. Consider this passage from the *Expositor's Bible Commentary*:

> The divine necessity for the sacrifice of the Son of Man does not excuse or mitigate the crime of betrayal. Divine sovereignty and human responsibility are both involved in Judas' treason, the one effecting salvation and bringing redemption history to its fulfillment, the other answering the promptings of an evil heart.[2]

We are never victims of some sort of sovereignty game. We always have a choice as to what we will treasure and value most. Because Judas treasured money over ministry and the Son of Man, he was an ideal candidate to fulfill the prophecies of Jesus' betrayal.

In order to ensure that we never fall into the trap of loving money more than ministry, let us always remember the words of Timothy:

> True religion with contentment is great wealth. After all, we didn't bring anything with us when we came into the world, and we certainly cannot carry anything with us when we die. So if we have enough food and clothing, let us be content. But people who long to be rich fall into temptation and are trapped by many foolish and harmful desires that plunge them into ruin and destruction. For the love of money is at the root of all kinds of evil. And some people, craving money, have wandered from the faith and pierced themselves with many sorrows. (1 Timothy 6:6–10)

HOLDING HIS HAND

Although I may value money, do I treasure it more than my relationships with other people? More than my relationship with God? Why or why not?

_____

_____

_____

Did Judas have to hang himself to absolve his guilt, or would God have been merciful to him if he had been "repentant" rather than simply "remorseful"? Why do I believe the way I do?

_____

_____

_____

If the love of money has been an issue for me, how can I combat the spirit of greed? What is the opposite of greed, and am I willing to move in this direction?

_____

_____

_____

Sovereign Lord,

_Let me never value money more than ministry, for the riches
I store up on earth will someday become ruins, whereas the
riches I store up in heaven will remain treasures forever.
Cleanse me of any greed that is in my heart, and replace it
with a spirit of charity and generosity toward You and others.
In Jesus' name. Amen._

COMMITTED FRIEND
OR CRAFTY FOE?

Daily reading: 2 Samuel 13

Key passage: Now Amnon had a very crafty friend—his cousin Jonadab. He was the son of David's brother Shimea. One day Jonadab said to Amnon, "What's the trouble? Why should the son of a king look so dejected morning after morning?"

So Amnon told him, "I am in love with Tamar, Absalom's sister."

"Well," Jonadab said, "I'll tell you what to do. Go back to bed and pretend you are sick. When your father comes to see you, ask him to let Tamar come and prepare some food for you. Tell him you'll feel better if she feeds you." (2 Samuel 13:3–5)

I don't know if there's a more disturbing thought than the idea that a brother could rape his own sister. Even more disheartening is Amnon's rejection of Tamar's offer to marry him as an attempt to "correct" the defilement she has experienced. However, our focus today isn't going to be on Amnon, but on Jonadab, because I believe his sin is one that we are far more likely to commit without conscious awareness of the damage we could do in someone else's life.

Second Samuel 13 is the only chapter in the Bible that mentions Jonadab. He is commemorated in such a way that none of us would want to be remembered—for his craftiness (see 2 Samuel 13:3). When he sees his cousin and friend Amnon looking dejected day after day, Jonadab inquires as to the problem. He seems concerned for his buddy. So far so good. Amnon responds that he is in love with his half sister, Tamar—understandable, as she is a beautiful woman (and it wasn't unusual during those times to marry a half brother or half sister, as was the case with Abraham and Sarah).

But then Jonadab plants some inappropriate ideas in Amnon's head about how he can manipulate the situation to his favor. Granted, Jonadab doesn't tell Amnon to rape Tamar. And we could interpret this passage to mean that Jonadab was only encouraging his friend to set the stage to talk to Tamar, woo her, and win her heart. However, there's nothing that would have kept Amnon from doing these things already, for he was free to interact with his half sister in such a way. Because this passage highlights Jonadab's craftiness, I believe he was encouraging Amnon to create an opportunity to get Tamar alone with him behind closed doors so he could have his way with her.

If Jonadab had been a true, godly friend and genuinely concerned about his cousin's happiness, I don't think he would have given him such bad advice. Jonadab should have realized that if Amnon violated his sister in such a way, she would serve as a constant reminder to him of his heinous behavior. Sure enough, after his dreadful deed, Amnon hates his sister "even more than he had loved her" (2 Samuel 13:15). Whereas before, Amnon most likely had the bedroom door locked so he could keep Tamar inside, now he insists that it be locked in order to keep her out.

Not only did Jonadab's bad advice prompt Amnon to rape his sister and destroy any possibility of their being together in an acceptable union, it also eventually led to Amnon's death at the hands of Tamar's brother, Absalom, who wanted revenge. As happy as we may be to read of Amnon's death after what he did to Tamar, I wonder how this story would have ended had Jonadab steered his friend down the straight-and-narrow path rather than down such a crooked one.

In Proverbs 18:24 we read, "There are 'friends' who destroy each other, but a real friend sticks closer than a brother." Are you the kind of friend who lifts others onto higher moral ground or the kind who lets others fall in whatever direction they choose? Have there been times when you've been a bad example or given ungodly or questionable advice? Or have you been the unfortunate recipient of poor advice from a so-called friend?

As I read this account and recognized Jonadab's part in this wicked plot, I was convicted of times when I have been guilty of similar doings, especially in my younger days. Rather than convincing a girlfriend that it was wrong and dangerous for her to sneak around with her boyfriend, I covered for her and lied to her parents, saying she was with me when actually she was with the guy they didn't approve of. Had he raped her, or if they had been killed while out together, how would I have felt? I shudder at the thought. And although never a drinker myself, I'm horrified by the handful of times I believed a friend or relative when she said, "Oh, I'm fine to drive," after she'd had a couple of drinks. If they'd been hurt in an accident or, worse, hurt someone else, I'm sure I would have carried that burden of guilt along with them.

The next time someone looks to you for advice, before you open your mouth, stop and ask yourself how Jesus would counsel that person. Remember, as the bride of Christ, you represent Him to others. Or even if your friend doesn't ask for advice, if you see her heading down a destructive path, don't buy the lie that it's "none of your business." A friend makes it her business to look out for the best interests of another friend. As children of God, we are to be our sisters' keepers whenever necessary.

HOLDING HIS HAND

Can you remember a time you gave (or received) poor advice to (or from) a friend? If so, what was the outcome? In a worst-case scenario, what could the outcome have been?

_____

_____

_____

Do you believe that as the bride of Christ you have a right to lovingly make other people's safety and wise choices your business? Why or why not?

_____

_____

_____

If a trusted, honest-intentioned friend approached you, waving a red flag and alerting you to a concern she has about your behavior, how would you respond? Would you be offended, or would you listen to what she has to say? Why?

_____

_____

_____

Dear Lord,

You have given us tremendous responsibility to be keepers of our brothers and sisters. Help us not to take this responsibility lightly, nor be fearful of their response. Instead, let us fear and obey You as You guide us in the matter. May we always be the kind of friend who lifts others up to a higher moral ground and spurs them on to live a happier, healthier lifestyle. Amen.

THE ULTIMATE
BAD-HAIR DAY

Daily reading: 2 Samuel 14:1–15:14; 18:1–18

Key passage: So Absalom went to Hebron. But while he was there, he sent secret messengers to every part of Israel to stir up a rebellion against the king. "As soon as you hear the trumpets," his message read, "you will know that Absalom has been crowned king in Hebron." He took two hundred men from Jerusalem with him as guests, but they knew nothing of his intentions. While he was offering the sacrifices, he sent for Ahithophel, one of David's counselors who lived in Giloh. Soon many others also joined Absalom, and the conspiracy gained momentum.
(2 Samuel 15:9–12)

While David was a man after God's own heart, he had many sons who didn't share his character qualities. We talked of one yesterday—Amnon, who raped his half sister—and today we read the tragic account of Absalom. While he was Tamar's hero for avenging her rape and taking her into his household, he eventually became a thorn in the side of his father and a falling star in the kingdom of Israel.

The Bible notes Absalom for being handsome and having gorgeous locks of hair. If you'll recollect from our reading about Samson, refusing to cut one's hair was usually a sign of the Nazirite vow a person had taken. However, Absalom made no such vow. I suspect his long hair was more a symbol of his haughtiness than his holiness. Filled with vanity and pride over his exceptional good looks, Absalom's heart proved not to be nearly as attractive, and it was ultimately his hair—his pride and vanity—that led to his demise.

Here's the story. Upon killing Amnon, Absalom flees to his grandfather's house in Geshur. After three years, David begins to long for his son's return, and Joab (and Joab's hired actress) finally convinces him to bring Absalom back from Geshur. However, David still won't welcome Absalom, although David's reasoning is unclear.

Perhaps as a result of his father's shunning him, Absalom torches Joab's field to get the king's attention. He wants to see his father and says, "If he finds me guilty of anything, then let him execute me" (2 Samuel 14:32). Absalom seems willing to face the consequences of killing his half brother if it means he will get to see his father. David finally concedes to Joab and Absalom's request, and after five years of estrangement, Absalom bows low to the king and kisses him.

As the story plays on, however, we see this kiss as more a betrayal (like Judas' kiss) than a blessing, for after this, Absalom begins plotting and scheming ways to usurp David's authority. In an attempt to make his father look bad (and to make himself look even better), Absalom resorts to lies, flattery, and false promises at the city gate. He wins the hearts of many people, hoping ultimately to steal the throne away from his father. After four years of campaigning in such a way, Absalom makes his strategic move. He sends his followers throughout Israel with the message, "As soon as you hear the trumpets...you will know that Absalom has been crowned king in Hebron" (2 Samuel 15:10).

Recognizing that Absalom's good looks and charm have deceived and wooed the people, and that his son's conspiracy is gaining momentum, David flees the palace and devises a plan of counterattack. However, he instructs his army to "deal gently with young Absalom" (2 Samuel 18:5). If we remember that David has already lost one infant son because of his sin with Bathsheba and then lost his son Amnon when Absalom killed him, we can better understand why David doesn't want Absalom killed.

David's soldiers, more experienced at riding horseback and sidestepping the inherent dangers of riding through trees, eventually overtake Absalom's less-experienced riders. While Absalom is fleeing, his hair gets caught in a tree branch, jerking him off his mule. Joab receives the report that Absalom is trapped and dangling from the tree, and in spite of David's plea, Joab puts three swords through Absalom's heart. Ten of Joab's armor bearers join in to complete the task. Then a trumpet sounds, not as a symbol of Absalom's being crowned king as he had intended, but as a symbol of the king's traitor being brought to justice.

Absalom's somber story prompts us to do a heart check in relation to those God has placed in authority over us. What is your attitude toward those in the workplace who have higher-ranking positions than you? Do you respect their judgment and submit to their authority, or do you whisper behind their backs with co-workers about their ineptness? What about your pastor? Do you value his theological opinions and leadership, or do you stir up gossip about his lack of pastoral abilities? And how about your husband? Do you respect his leadership (even if you don't particularly agree with it), or do you undermine his authority by being disrespectful to him? Or worse, do you talk disrespectfully about him to your children when he is not around?

Whenever I hear someone say something ill or tacky about someone in authority, do you know what my standard reaction is? I make a mental note: *Don't trust this person. If she talks about someone else like this to me, she will likely talk like this about me to someone else.*

God grants us the respect and favor of others when we earn it. We don't earn it by making another person look bad. We earn it when we show the proper respect, submission, and appreciation toward those in authority over us.

HOLDING HIS HAND

Have I ever walked in Absalom's shoes, tearing down the character of another in order to get ahead and fulfill my own agenda? If so, why did I feel such a need?

_____

_____

_____

Have I ever walked in David's shoes, feeling as if someone was intentionally trying to destroy my reputation in order to gain favor for themselves? If so, how did that make me feel?

_____

_____

_____

What do I need to do in order to show the proper respect to those in authority over me? to my supervisors at work? to my pastor? to my husband?

_____

_____

_____

Lord God,

You are the divine Creator, desiring proper order in all things, from the vast universe right down to our personal relationships. Teach us how to submit, respect, and appreciate those You have placed in authority over us, and help us be humble and responsible authority figures to those over whom we are given in leadership. Amen.

FROM RICHES TO RAGS

Daily reading: 1 Kings 11

Key passage: The LORD was very angry with Solomon, for his heart had turned away from the LORD, the God of Israel, who had appeared to him twice. He had warned Solomon specifically about worshiping other gods, but Solomon did not listen to the LORD's command. So now the LORD said to him, "Since you have not kept my covenant and have disobeyed my laws, I will surely tear the kingdom away from you and give it to one of your servants. But for the sake of your father, David, I will not do this while you are still alive. I will take the kingdom away from your son. And even so, I will let him be king of one tribe, for the sake of my servant David and for the sake of Jerusalem, my chosen city." (1 Kings 11:9–13)

King Solomon's end has to be the most bewildering and disheartening of all the biblical characters'. While there is no indication that he lost any of his financial wealth, his was still a riches-to-rags story.

You likely know that Solomon was one of the wisest and wealthiest men who ever lived, because the Lord bestowed such favor on him. He had far more money, respect, and honor than any other king in history. Royalty from faraway lands sought his wisdom and were amazed at the riches Israel had amassed under his leadership. Solomon had the vision and the resources given him to build an enormous, elaborate temple in which the Lord would make His dwelling place. What more could he ask from the Lord?

But despite all that God had given Solomon, he did not heed what God had asked of him, and this led to his downfall. In Deuteronomy 17:16–17, God commanded three things of kings: (1) that they not build up an inordinate amount of horses, for God wanted them to rely on His strength, not the strength of larger armies; (2) that they not accumulate vast amounts of silver and gold (however, God could grant it to them, as He did to Solomon); and (3) that kings not take multiple wives (nor wives from other nations) so that their hearts wouldn't be turned away from God. Solomon ignored this last command altogether, as evidenced by his seven hundred wives and three hundred concubines.

While Solomon may have been wise, he was foolish when it came to women. Having multiple wives and concubines must have posed major distractions. Living intimately with hundreds of foreign women left him incredibly vulnerable to the temptation of being unfaithful to his God.

Solomon's idolatry and rebellion against God's command led to some serious consequences for him, his heirs, and the nation of Israel. In 1 Kings 11, Ahijah the prophet approaches Jeroboam, a rebel leader who was one of King Solomon's officials. Ahijah takes his new cloak from around his shoulders and tears in into twelve rags. The prophet then gives ten of these rags to Jeroboam, saying that the Lord is about to tear the kingdom from the hand of Solomon and give ten of its tribes to Jeroboam because of Solomon's idolatry. However, in His mercy and in order to remain true to His promise to Solomon's father, David, God pledges to maintain Solomon's leadership over the one Israelite tribe of Judah. (The twelfth tribe of Levi is led by the Lord Himself.) When Solomon hears all of this, he attempts to kill Jeroboam out of jealousy but fails. After a forty-year reign, Solomon dies a materially wealthy but spiritually bankrupt man.

I don't think Solomon woke up one day, saying, "Hey! I think I'll commit idolatry today and go worship a few foreign gods!" No doubt his heart was gradually led astray by his foreign wives. Few of us intend to fall away from our devotion to the Lord. We don't wake up and say, "I think I'll flirt with my cute co-worker over lunch today, watch some mindless television this afternoon, and get into some occult practices by sundown!" Such things happen gradually. We begin by being flattered by a man's compliments. Then we choose to go out of our way to encounter him, fishing for more affirmation from him in place of looking to God for it. Rather than do our Bible study, we sit down to watch a seemingly innocent movie, and when the content becomes questionable, we slide our conscience under the living room rug. We intend to be more regular in prayer and church attendance, but we allow our lives to be so filled with other, less important things that our busyness overshadows spiritual matters. Slowly, one day at a time, we fall further and further away from God without realizing it.

But it doesn't have to be this way. By intentionally practicing spiritual disciplines, such as reading God's Word and talking with Him daily, and an occasional heart check with an accountability friend, pastor, or mentor, we can rest assured that our lives will never become spiritual riches-to-rags stories.

HOLDING HIS HAND

Is there something that God may be trying to show me about my life through the example of King Solomon? If so, what might it be?

_____

_____

_____

_____

_____

Are there activities in my day that, if left unchecked, could become sin or even idolatry? If so, what are they, and how can I remedy the situation?

_____

_____

_____

_____

_____

Do I spend regular time connecting with God through Scripture reading, meditation, and prayer, or do I allow other things to inhibit my devotion to Christ? How do I feel about my answer?

_____

_____

_____

_____

_____

> *Lord God,*
>
> *None of us intends to fall away from You, but so many things in this world can be incredibly alluring. Keep us from being lulled into a spiritual slumber, Lord! Help us maintain a deep, passionate connection with You, for You alone are worthy of our worship and complete devotion. Amen.*

IN-LAW OR OUTLAW?

Daily reading: Genesis 30:25–31:55

Key passage: Twenty years I have been with you, and all that time I cared for your sheep and goats so they produced healthy offspring.… I worked for you through the scorching heat of the day and through cold and sleepless nights. Yes, twenty years—fourteen of them earning your two daughters, and six years to get the flock. And you have reduced my wages ten times! In fact, except for the grace of God—the God of my grandfather Abraham, the awe-inspiring God of my father, Isaac—you would have sent me off without a penny to my name. But God has seen your cruelty and my hard work. That is why he appeared to you last night and vindicated me. (Genesis 31:38, 40–42)

If it's true that "what goes around comes around," then the deception that Jacob dealt his brother and father when he stole Esau's birthright and blessing came back to him tenfold through his father-in-law, Laban. Earlier, we saw Laban tricking Jacob into seven years of additional work after sending Leah into Jacob's wedding chamber rather than Rachel. When Jacob rebuked his father-in-law for playing such a trick, Laban responded, "It's not our custom to marry off a younger daughter ahead of the firstborn.... Wait until the bridal week is over, and you can have Rachel, too—that is, if you promise to work another seven years for me" (Genesis 29:26–27).

What game is Laban playing here? Is he concerned that his firstborn daughter will become an old maid if she doesn't get married before her younger sister? Perhaps, but it seems more likely that Laban wants to get Jacob to work for him for twice as long as Jacob had initially committed.

Years later, Jacob senses that the party is over and it's time for him to return home with his wives and children. He is very aboveboard with his father-in-law, being careful not to stoop to Laban's level. He has paid his dues, working fourteen years to pay the bride price for his two brides. He wants Laban's blessing as he moves into a new season of life with his family.

However, his father-in-law practically begs Jacob to stay, offering to pay him whatever Jacob feels he is owed. Again, we have to wonder about Laban's motive. Does he fear that he will miss his daughters and grandchildren once they are gone, or is Laban's greed at work here, since he claims that God has revealed to him that he's being blessed *through Jacob* (see Genesis 30:27)? If I had to place a bet, I'd put my money on the latter. Why am I so suspicious of Laban? Because when Jacob offers to stay for a while longer in exchange for the speckled, spotted, and dark-colored sheep, Laban turns around and removes all the livestock fitting that description. Where does Laban put them? He gives them to his sons and sends them on a three-day journey to make sure Jacob can't get to them. He attempts to make it impossible for Jacob to build a sizable flock of his own.

At this point, I'm sure Jacob was at his wit's end with his trickster father-in-law. Remember, he had been tending the sheep all along. He knew approximately what percentage of the flock was pure white and what percentage was dappled or dark colored. When he got up that morning and discovered only white sheep in the pasture, he had to know he had been duped once again. However, God blessed Jacob's unique breeding procedures, and Jacob became exceedingly wealthy, all thanks owed to his heavenly Father rather than to his greedy father-in-law.

When Laban and his sons discover that their scheme to cheat Jacob has backfired, the sons grumble, "Jacob has robbed our father!... All his wealth has been gained at our father's expense" (Genesis 31:1). Talk about the pot calling the kettle black! Who's attempting to rob whom? All this makes Jacob realize the time has come to move back to his homeland. Not even Laban's own daughters put up a fight over the idea of leaving, for they know that their father had tried to cheat them out of their own inheritance. Perhaps this is why, as they are leaving, Rachel steals her father's prized possessions—his household gods. Since God never appears to rebuke Rachel for her theft, it poses the question: *was this God's way of giving Laban a dose of his own medicine?*

Once Jacob and his family make their quick getaway, Laban comes chasing after them. He questions Jacob as to why he would sneak away without allowing him to send them off properly. Are you thinking what I'm thinking? *Duh! Because Jacob has your number by now, buddy!* Laban has cheated Jacob over and over, coerced him into staying longer and longer, manipulated him into working harder and harder. He's reduced Jacob's wages ten times and seems to have a hard time keeping any promise made to his son-in-law. I think it's safe to say that you and I would also want to run away from an outlaw in-law like Laban.

While none of us would ever want to be cheated by someone, *have we been guilty of cheating someone else?* Sadly, it can be a huge temptation, even for Christians. As I made hundreds of copies of my first manuscript on Teen Mania's copy machine, I occasionally had thoughts like, *No one knows how many copies you are making, Shannon. It's all in the name of ministry, and that's what this organization is all about. They've got far more money than you do. A few free copies won't hurt them.* But deep in my heart, I knew it wasn't just "a few copies." It was a matter of morals...ethics...principles I knew to be true, such as "what goes around comes around," and you "reap what you sow" (Galatians

6:7). Was I willing to sell my integrity for five bucks here and ten bucks there? No way! I paid for every copy with a happy heart and my head held high.

Is there any amount of money that would be worth selling your integrity for? Whether for five dollars or five million dollars, the bride of Christ must resist stooping to Laban's level. A person's integrity—*your integrity*—is absolutely priceless.

HOLDING HIS HAND

Have I ever put a price on my integrity, selling out my morals and convictions for a little financial gain? If so, how?

_____

_____

_____

_____

Is there an organization or a person that I have cheated in the past? Do I have the courage and conviction to ask for forgiveness and offer restitution? Why or why not?

_____

_____

_____

_____

Do I believe we all reap what we sow? Based on the seeds I've sown, what kind of harvest can I expect to reap? Why?

_____

_____

_____

_____

Beautiful Savior,

So often we can be tempted to try to get ahead at the expense of others. Help us to banish this thought whenever it comes into our brains! Reveal to us the enormous value of character and integrity and of trusting in You alone for our provision and financial gain. Amen.

DRIVEN TO DISTRACTION

Daily reading: Nehemiah 4; 6

Key passage: When Sanballat, Tobiah, Geshem the Arab, and the rest of our enemies found out that I had finished rebuilding the wall and that no gaps remained—though we had not yet hung the doors in the gates—Sanballat and Geshem sent me a message asking me to meet them at one of the villages in the plain of Ono. But I realized they were plotting to harm me, so I replied by sending this message to them: "I am doing a great work! I cannot stop to come and meet with you."

Four times they sent the same message, and each time I gave the same reply. (Nehemiah 6:1–4)

*C*all it coincidence, but the theme I'm currently writing about often becomes a central theme in my own life. Sure enough, all week long I've been driven to distraction! While I had intended to write about Nehemiah on a Tuesday, I finally sat down to my laptop Saturday evening. I had allowed myself to get caught up in anything and everything that week—anything, that is, except writing. Whether it was phone calls, e-mails, grocery lists, pet or child-care needs, household chores, carpool, teacher meetings, errands, or doctor visits, something always seemed to beckon me away from where I needed to be—in meditation, in prayer, in study, and in my office writing.

As you've probably noticed by now, I sometimes see a particular strength in a biblical character that I only wish I had. Nehemiah's ability to remain focused on his God-given task is a trait I can only wish to emulate more often.

When Nehemiah discovers that the walls of Jerusalem are decaying, he decides not to worry about it, complain about it, or blame anyone for it. Instead, he does something about the problem. Nehemiah is incredibly insightful as to what it will take to complete this massive project, and he is willing to roll up both his physical and spiritual sleeves to get the work done. Rather than pray and expect God to do all the work, or have his men do all the work and neglect calling upon God, Nehemiah covers both bases. He incorporates both spiritual and physical strategies, praying earnestly to God as well as scheduling workers around the clock.

However, a couple of people don't want to see the wall rebuilt, namely Sanballat and Tobiah. On numerous occasions, they try to distract Nehemiah, insulting him, laughing at him, threatening him, and trying to lure him away from his mission. But Nehemiah is no dummy. He senses that these men have less-than-sincere motives. Although many workers fear these bullies, Nehemiah isn't one of them. Why? Because he fears only the Lord. During the entire fifty-two-day project, Nehemiah doesn't allow anyone to distract him, for he refuses to let God down. Notice that Nehemiah also feels no need to expend the time and energy required to handle these bullies. He leaves that up to God and saves his strength for the task at hand. Wise move, Nehemiah. Keep your nose to the grindstone and "git 'r done!"

Oh, how I wish I had such fierce resolve! Still, I have managed to pick up a couple of tools that I try to keep in my tool belt. First, I've learned that the most important things in life need to be my most important priorities of the day, and my spiritual health is certainly my most important priority. While I don't subscribe to the idea that you have to have your Quiet Time in the wee hours of the morning before you do anything else (most of us at least need some caffeine and a shower first), I do feel that we have to make a firm appointment with God and keep it, just as we would keep an appointment with the president of the United States. After all, He's more important than anyone in our lives, and we don't just *find* time to commune with God—we have to *make* time.

Second, I've learned that people and things will practically stand in line in order to distract me when I am having my Quiet Time. We have to take control of how we spend our time. While we can't make the world stop interrupting us, we can commit to some focused time with God. I can turn the phone ringer off and let the answering machine take calls, close out my e-mail screen, and put a sign on the front door that says, "Shh! Meeting with God in progress. Please do not disturb." My FedEx man and Avon lady may think I'm a little weird, but they respect my wishes and leave their packages at the door.

God may never ask us to rebuild a wall around an entire city, but He does assign us specific roles to fill. The most important role God wants us to fill is that of His beloved bride. So invest time each day in tearing down any walls that separate you from your Savior, such as busyness and distractions. Remember the old saying, "If the devil can't make you bad, he'll make you busy!" Just as Nehemiah diligently built a wall for God, diligently build a bridge to God, connecting the two of you.

HOLDING HIS HAND

Is my relationship with God the priority in my life that it needs to be? Why or why not?

_____

_____

_____

What is the biggest distraction or unnecessary time waster in my day? Do I have control over it? Why or why not?

_____

_____

_____

How can I exercise more control over my day so that I can make intimate time with God the priority that I'd like it to be?

_____

_____

_____

Precious Lord,

We long to feel closer to You, but sometimes the longing to check everything off our to-do lists or to respond to everyone else's expectations distracts us from this mission. Slow us down, Lord, and show us how to create healthy boundaries around our time and energies. Draw us into Your presence with a gentle reminder of just how much we benefit from special time spent with You. In Jesus' name. Amen.

WHEN THE COCK CROWS

Daily reading: Matthew 16:13–19; 26:31–35, 57–75; John 21:15–19

Key passage: Peter said, "I swear by God, I don't know the man." And immediately the rooster crowed. Suddenly, Jesus' words flashed through Peter's mind: "Before the rooster crows, you will deny me three times." And he went away, crying bitterly. (Matthew 26:74–75)

---

*O*f the twelve disciples, Peter was surely the most fearless and outspoken one of the bunch. If he were born in our era, I suspect he'd be the toddler who pretends to be the teacher, lining up all of his stuffed animals to tell them what to do. He'd be the college student who consistently raises his hand, not just to eagerly answer every question, but also to help the professor get his own facts straight. As an adult, he would have campaign posters all over the country—Peter for President!

Indeed, Peter could be the poster child for the type-A personality. But God didn't create Peter to live in our era. He created Peter to walk the earth at the time of Christ. Why? So that this great leader could launch one of the most important ongoing missions of all time. But as fearless and outspoken as Peter was, he proved by his actions that every great leader has limits.

We pick up the story in Matthew 26 during the Last Supper, where Jesus predicts that before the night is over, all the disciples will scatter from His presence and desert Him. In response Peter boldly declares, "Even if everyone else deserts you, I never will" (verse 33). But Jesus sees past Peter's courage to the cowardice within and replies, "The truth is, this very night, before the rooster crows, you will deny me three times" (verse 34).

True to form, Peter argues. The Rabbi doesn't have His facts straight. What He is saying isn't true at all. "Not even if I have to die with you! I will never deny you!" insists Peter (verse 35), leading the other disciples to agree with his passionate profession.

It's not long, however, before we see Peter in a very different position. Jesus has been arrested, and rather than sticking by His Master's side, Peter is merely "following far behind" (verse 58). Three different times he is approached by someone inquiring about his connection with the accused. And just as Jesus predicted, Peter denies even knowing the man he had pledged to die with if necessary. The cock crows, and Peter sheds his pride along with many tears of bitterness.

You'd think that God would be finished with someone who won't even claim he knows the Christ, right? What good could Peter possibly be to Jesus now that he has denied Him three times? However, God is certainly not through with Peter. In many ways, this was just the beginning. Having been humbled, Peter surely recognizes the magnitude of Christ's commitment versus the smallness of his own. With the heaping helping of pride now swallowed and digested, Peter is in a better position to be used by God to an even greater degree.

But God knew that Peter's authority had to be divinely reinstated in order for Peter to have the confidence to carry out his calling. So after Jesus is resurrected, He asks Peter not once, but three times, "Do you love me?" (once for each time Peter denied Him) (John 21:15–17). Each time Peter replies, "Lord, you know I love you," but his declaration of devotion is not nearly as forceful or as prideful as before. Peter seems to be painfully aware of the limitations of his previous proclamations. Jesus is also aware of Peter's awkwardness over the whole betrayal thing, and this public exchange between Him and Peter is intended to be a reinstatement of Peter as a leader of Christ's church as well as an act of reconciliation between the two of them. Jesus then prophesies that even though Peter wasn't willing to follow Jesus to the cross before, he will follow Him to his own cross in the future.

What can we learn from Peter's denial and reinstatement? Regardless of our sincere intentions to follow Christ, there may come a time (or there may have already been a time) when we recognize that our love for Him has its limitations. I can recall little things I did as a younger Christian that I now hang my head in shame over—stacking my Bible underneath my textbooks so fellow students wouldn't think I was a goody two-shoes, putting my cross necklace under my T-shirt so the cute guy on campus wouldn't think I was a "Jesus freak," or committing to the Lord that I would spend all day fasting, only to stick a spoon into the ice cream carton before noon.

Are there times when your commitment to Christ falls short? Or when you are somehow ashamed of your faith or fearful of what people will think of you if they realize you are a disciple of Christ? If so, remember how Jesus gently responded to Peter's denial. He feels the same way about you. He wants you, His beloved bride, to receive His free gift of forgiveness, to be reinstated to a position of spiritual authority in His kingdom, and to have your intimate relationship with Him fully restored. All you have to do is humbly ask.

HOLDING HIS HAND

Have there been times in my life when I have denied my association with Jesus Christ? Have I ever felt ashamed to admit that I'm a Christian? Why or why not?

_____

_____

_____

If God could use Peter in spite of his denial, can He use me in order to expand His church? If so, how can He use even my shortcomings for His glory?

_____

_____

_____

Do I believe with all my heart that Jesus has sympathy for our weaknesses and offers us nothing but unconditional love, mercy, and grace when our love for Him proves to be not-so-limitless? Why or why not?

_____

_____

_____

Gracious, loving Father,

You deserve nothing but 100 percent commitment and devotion, yet few of us ever feel as if we even get close to that mark. We ask You to place a rock-solid assurance deep in our hearts that our sins do not disqualify us from Your service. Help us to embrace Your forgiveness and the knowledge that we have been fully reinstated and restored in our relationship with You. Amen.

Are You Ready to Take Another Step Closer?

*I*sn't God's Word addictive? The more you read and come to understand about the Bible, the more you long to know the author intimately. That's the effect that love letters have on readers. Our eyes long to devour every sentiment over and over, searching for nuances and signs of our admirer's affections toward us. I hope that's the impact these devotionals are having on you so far. I pray you are feeling completely loved and completely forgiven by our adoring heavenly Bridegroom!

Are you now ready to feel completely blessed by Him? If so, I invite you to join me in the next devotional in the series:

Completely Blessed: Discovering God's Extraordinary Gifts

In *Completely Blessed,* we'll examine some of the parables and teachings in the New Testament that reveal the lavishness of God's generosity toward His beloved bride. You'll be awestruck at the passion and creativity He's poured into fashioning special tokens of His overwhelming affection toward us. Of course, we'll hold His hand on a daily basis once again, cultivating a heart of gratitude for both God's presence and His special presents in our lives.

If you love opening gifts like I do, join me as we unwrap some of the most extravagant gifts a girl can imagine!

A Note from Shannon

Are you looking for a unique idea for a women's retreat? An extraordinary experience for women of all ages, from all walks of life? Drive home the encouraging principles presented in this book.

Consider hosting a *Completely His* event that allows women to experience the joy of committing their "bridal love" to Jesus Christ, their heavenly Bridegroom.

Because a bride doesn't feel like a bride until she walks down the aisle wearing white, this event resembles a wedding ceremony in many ways, and yet is unlike any other—a sweet foretaste of the great wedding supper of the Lamb that is yet to come for all of us someday!

My ministry assistants and I have coordinated these events the past several years for groups as small as ten and as large as four hundred.

Participants describe the experience as "powerfully real" (Lyn, age 52), "incomparable—no wedding will ever compare to this experience until Jesus returns" (Tracy, age 20), and "life transforming" (Samantha, age 38).

Go to www.shannonethridge.com for plenty of creative ideas, products, and downloadable forms to help you coordinate your own *Completely His* women's event.

Notes

Day 3

1. The Bible Encyclopedia, "Birthright," iLumina Bible Software, Tyndale, 2003.

Day 6

1. Kenneth L. Barker and John R. Kohlenberger III, *The Expositor's Bible Commentary*, Abridged Edition: New Testament (Grand Rapids, MI: Zondervan, 1994), 440.

Day 7

1. Amy Grant, "Lead Me On," *Lead Me On* (Myrrh/A&M Records, 1988).

Day 9

1. Bob Carlisle, "We Fall Down," *Stories from the Heart* (Diadem Records, 1998).

Day 10

1. Daniel DeNoon, "When Are You Too Old for Pregnancy?" *New England Journal of Medicine*, November 3, 2004. www.webmd.com/content/Article/96/ 103758.htm?pagenumber=1.

Day 13

1. Frank Sinatra, "My Way," lyrics by P. Anka, J. Revaux, G. Thibault, C. Francois.

Day 17

1. Portions of this devotional were adapted from the preface of Shannon Ethridge's first book, *Words of Wisdom for Women at the Well* (Ontario, Canada: Essence, 2003), 10–13 (available at www.shannon ethridge.com).

Day 22

1. Kenneth L. Barker and John R. Kohlenberger III, *The Expositor's Bible Commentary*, Abridged Edition: New Testament (Grand Rapids, MI: Zondervan, 1994), 322.

Day 24

1. Joanna Weaver, *Having a Mary Heart in a Martha World* (Colorado Springs, CO: WaterBrook, 2002), 160.
2. Kenneth L. Barker and John R. Kohlenberger III, *The Expositor's Bible Commentary*, Abridged Edition: New Testament (Grand Rapids, MI: Zondervan, 1994), 119.

TOPICAL INDEX

Scripture Index